# INTERRELIGIOUS STUDIES AND SECONDARY EDUCATION

## Pedagogies and Practices
## for Living and Learning
## in a Religiously Plural World

*Edited by*
Lucinda Mosher
Christine Gallagher
Axel M. Oaks Takács

*Interreligious Studies Press* is an imprint of *Interreligious Studies Media*, a non-profit whose mission provides spaces for the distribution of critical, constructive, and cutting-edge scholarship and pedagogies related to the field of interreligious/interfaith studies and its adjacent disciplines. These spaces include the *Journal of Interreligious Studies, Interreligious Studies Press*, webinars, and other digital and print learning materials

*Institute for Islamic, Christian, and Jewish Studies (ICJS)* is an independent, educational nonprofit organization working to model a new conversation in the public square that affirms religious diversity in the United States.

*Interreligious Studies and Secondary Education: Pedagogies and Practices for Living and Learning in a Religiously Plural World*
First Edition
Copyright © 2025 by *Interreligious Studies Media* and *Institute for Islamic, Christian, and Jewish Studies*

Published by
*Interreligious Studies Press* and *Institute for Islamic, Christian, and Jewish Studies*
c/o Hebrew College
1860 Washington Street
Newton, Massachusetts 02466
irstudies.org

Cover design by Barrie S. Mosher and Angela Cava

Printed in the United States of America

ISBN 979-8-9926310-0-5

9 798992 631005

# CONTENTS

# INTRODUCTION

"It is kind of like trying to teach Trigonometry to students who do not really understand what 'x' means in Algebra," explained the instructor for an undergraduate intro-level World Christianity course. He had to cover such disparate topics as the relationship between Christian and Jewish traditions (historically and today), the impact of Paul (the New Testament author) on the early Jesus movement, and how Christian traditions and practices are shaped when embodied, emplaced, and enacted in Buddhist-majority regions of the world (for instance). So, the analogy he offered was apt. Where do you even *begin* when students lack basic literacy regarding the category "religion" itself, much less regarding the basic building blocks for understanding the practices and beliefs of the diverse traditions of the world?

Where math, science, and literature are seen as central to K–12 education, religion—if not sidelined altogether—is at best sprinkled into some units of other subjects. Religiously affiliated K–12 institutions may give substantial attention to their own religion. Typically, it resembles catechesis; and when they do attend to "the World's Religions," rarely is it informed by insights from the academic disciplines of religious studies or interreligious studies. K–12 religiously affiliated extracurricular youth organizations may do a better job opening the eyes of students to the religious diversity of the world; but with the increase in religious disaffiliation in the North American context—and with the increase of polarizing and exclusive attitudes of those who remain religiously affiliated—those opportunities are few and far between.

Yet expanding opportunities for children and adolescents to learn about religion has great value. They become more aware of how religious traditions interact with each other and with secularity; and they embody that learning in the lived encounter with religiously diverse groups of people. In fact, becoming interreligiously literate, intelligent, and proficient *today* is a social and civic necessity, if there is to be a more just and equitable *tomorrow*.[1] In this introduction, we offer a brief overview of the place of *studying* religion in K–12 institutions and of *encountering* religious diversity in extracurricular youth organizations before proceeding to outline the origin and content of this volume.

Twenty-five years ago, Warren A. Nord and Charles C. Haynes claimed the emergence of a "New Consensus" in their book *Taking Religion Seriously Across the Curriculum*. Bolstered by statements from several governmental, educational, and curricular bodies,[2] Nord and Haynes concluded that the inclusion of religion in the K–12 public curriculum was essential for full engagement in civic and educational life.[3] They called for robust reforms in teacher education to give the "New Consensus" lasting impact.

Over the course of the nearly three decades since Nord and Haynes issued their assessment, the landscape of religious studies departments, religion in the United States, and K–12 education has taken on a very different look, yet the questions that animated their project persist. Some institutions have taken up their call for reforms with guidance, others continue to leave their teachers and administrators in the dark, while still others may perpetuate—intentionally or not—conservative Christian conceptions of religion and the (inferior) status of non-Christian traditions.[4]

The National Council for Social Studies (NCSS) has been a leader in the field. In 2000, following its earlier guidance, NCSS joined with the US Department of Education to share a document with every public school in the United States that affirmed an academic approach to teaching about religion. Here, "academic approach" is intended to distinguish a method of religious education that is *not* apologetic, proselytizing, indoctrinating, or otherwise devotional; it is based on rigorous academic standards employed by scholars of religion. In 2013, NCSS published the *College, Career, and Civic Life (C3) Framework for Social Studies State Standards: Guidance for Enhancing the Rigor of K-12 Civics, Economics, Geography, and History*. The C3 Framework revolutionized the field after more than a decade of devolution of social studies curriculum conversation thanks to the adoption of No Child Left Behind and Common Core standards. Many states continue to use C3 to frame and model their social studies standards, a feat for guidance that is a decade old.[5]

One of the greatest impacts on the C3 Framework has been the focus on inquiry across social studies curricula. Moving away from rote memorization and parroting of dates and facts, the Inquiry Arc invites educators to help hone students' skills in question asking, conclusion finding, and action planning: "the framework emphasizes the disciplinary concepts and practices that support students as they develop the capacity to know, analyze, explain, and argue about interdisciplinary challenges in our social world."[6]

In 2017, the NCSS updated the C3 Framework with *Religious Studies Companion Document to the C3 Framework*. The supplement aligns the inquiry model with religious studies; standards are offered that encourage students to use critical thinking skills regarding religious studies in the social studies classroom. It also advances and explains an academic rather than a devotional approach and emphasizes the importance of religious literacy for our globalized society.[7]

The *Religious Studies Companion Document for the C3 Framework* owes a great deal to the American Academy Religion (AAR) *Guidelines for Teaching about Religion in K–12 Public Schools*. The AAR warns against the rise of religious illiteracy. In advocating for a balanced and fair treatment of diverse religious perspectives in the classroom, *Guidelines* includes understanding the First Amendment's establishment clause and free exercise clause, as well as promoting a secular, neutral stance by public institutions.

The work toward "a new consensus" continues as a new generation tackles questions of religious literacy in K-12 education. In their assessment of the field, published in 2020, Benjamin Marcus, Kate Soules, and David Callaway call for the growing group of scholars and practitioners to work together to influence curricular and institutional work around religion in schools through resource gathering, research, outreach, policy building, and teacher education.[8] Many educators and scholars in this volume contribute to this growing body of work.

*Interreligious Studies and Secondary Education: Pedagogies and Practices for Living and Learning in a Religiously Plural World* is a collection of essays by educators and others who address multireligious concerns in their work with teenagers. It is offered as a resource to anyone who is interested in models and methods of cultivating multireligious fluency among teens. The impetus for this volume was "Growing in Spirit: Exploring Interreligious Education at the High School and Undergraduate Levels," a 2021 webinar sponsored by the *Journal of Interreligious Studies* and the *Association for Interreligious / Interfaith Studies* (and made possible by the Arthur Vining Davis Foundations). At the end of this event, the organizers noticed a disparity: the number of pedagogical strategies, best practices, theories, and educational materials for teaching interreligious studies in the undergraduate classroom had significantly increased and their quality improved over the past several years. Certificates, minors, majors, and courses in interreligious studies across North America were on the rise. This was a positive outcome. However, while there were a promising number of exceptional educators and community organizers spearheading interreligious literacy at the K–12 level, it lagged severely behind the undergraduate level. The primary culprit, of course, was not a lack of will or a dearth of outstanding educators and community organizers, but rather a structural failure to invest in religious and interreligious literacy for students and youth at the K–12 level.

Volumes on the theory, practice, and pedagogies of interreligious studies at the undergraduate and graduate level (including divinity schools and seminaries) are plentiful. These include, inter alia, *Interreligious/Interfaith Studies* (Beacon Press, 2018), *Critical Perspectives on Interreligious Education* (Brill, 2020), *Interreligious Studies* (Baylor University Press, 2020), *Deep Understanding for Divisive Times* (Interreligious Studies Press, 2020), *Decolonial Futures* (Lexington Books, 2021), *Interreligious Studies: An Introduction* (Cambridge University Press, 2023), and *Everyday Wisdom: Interreligious Studies in a Pluralistic World* (Fortress Academic, 2023). In addition, the *Journal of Interreligious Studies* dedicated Issue 36 to interfaith and interreligious pedagogies.[9] As is evident by this list, there is a relative dearth of scholarship on pedagogies and practices of teaching interreligiously at the secondary-education level and age-group, including activities led by community youth organizations. This volume seeks to begin to fill this lacuna.

Another impetus for this volume is the argument presented by Khyati Joshi in *White Christian Privilege: The Illusion of Religious Equality in America* (NYU Press, 2020). Joshi critically demonstrates the various ways in which Christian normativity shapes the external/structural and internal/attitudinal dimensions of societies within the United States. She connects Christianity with notions of Whiteness and argues that "White Christian supremacy in America is the product of a centuries-long project in which notions of White racial superiority and Christian religious superiority have augmented and magnified each other,"[10] creating legacies of systemic (legal and institutional) and ideological (attitudinal) religious and cultural oppression among minoritized groups. If the structural and attitudinal dimensions are to change, interreligious education for justice must take place at every level.

To that end, the *Journal of Interreligious Studies* sought to bring together in one volume exemplary voices from both secondary education and community organizations involved with adolescents around interreligious/interfaith teaching, understanding, and justice. For such a project, the Institute for Islamic, Christian, and Jewish Studies (ICJS) would be an excellent partner primarily because of the success of their outstanding Teachers Fellowship program. Most of the essayists in the resulting *Interreligious Studies and Secondary Education: Pedagogies and Practices for Living and Learning in a Religiously Plural World* are teachers in secondary schools—some of them public; others, religiously affiliated. Many have been participants in the ICJS Teachers Fellowship, the history and progress of which is described by Christine Gallagher in Chapter 1: "Education Eradicates Ignorance: The Institute for Islamic, Christian, and Jewish Studies' Teachers Fellowship." As Gallaher explains, middle- and high-school educators are often ill-equipped to teach about religion in their classrooms. To do so requires more than the standards and benchmarks given to them by administrators. The yearlong Teachers Fellowship program creates a professional learning community of educators. Together, they gain confidence in teaching about religion and look for opportunities to build religious literacy in their own lives and institutions. Reflective writing is an important component of this program. *Interreligious Studies and Secondary Education* offers a selection of those reflection pieces. It supplements them with essays by others who are wrestling with whether and how to incorporate work with teens on better understanding of religion(s). Each of the seventeen essays chosen for this volume concludes with prompts for further discussion or journaling.

Essays have been organized under four headings. Part I: "Theory," opens, as has already been noted, with an account by Christine Gallagher of the ICJS Teachers Fellowship program. It is followed by four chapters providing examples of processes of religion curriculum redesign in public and international schools. The four essays of Part II: "Practice" are accounts of actual educational models and instructional methods in action. Part III: "Religiously Affiliated School Settings" offers four reflections on experiences as teachers in Catholic or Quaker institutions, Part IV: "Outside and Beyond Secondary Education" provides three accounts of extracurricular or co-curricular projects, plus reflections on interfaith programs for recent high school graduates as they transition into college life. An afterword by Heather Miller Rubens, executive director of ICJS, provides an analytical framework that helps the reader appreciate the shifting positionality and identity of "the teacher."

The editors have located this opus in the arena of Interreligious Studies, defined as "an interdisciplinary, integrative academic field that promotes deep understanding of worldviews different from one's own and cultivates the dynamic link between theory and practice as it engages in critical investigation of relations between people (whether individuals or groups) who orient around 'religion' differently (howsoever religion be defined)."[11] Interreligious Studies is inherently multi-disciplinary. It gives pride of place to relational, intersectional, and dialogical approaches. It encourages wide (but not exclusive) use of comparative and critical methods. Its purposes include cultivation of religious literacy, promotion of dialogue, fostering of citizenship, and professional preparation for leadership in multireligious contexts.[12] While this volume's contributors are unlikely to think of themselves as practitioners, their methods, rationales, and outcomes fit here well. The field of Interreligious Studies, which is still in its adolescence, has spawned a number of books on philosophy and method, as mentioned above. *Interreligious Studies and Secondary Education: Pedagogies and Practices for Living and Learning in a Religiously Plural World* is the first volume in this field to focus on secondary education.

*Interreligious Studies and Secondary Education* seeks to motivate more teaching of and about religion across the secondary school curriculum. While social studies is an obvious K–12 subject in which to teach about religion, it is not the only space.[13] The American Academy of Religion makes a strong case for teaching about religion across disciplines as it explores historical, literary, traditions-based, and cultural studies approaches.[14] Against any call for more space for the study of religion or the employment of interreligious studies principles and practices in pre-college curricular and extracurricular settings, pushback is likely. Some would object to allocation of time and resources to teaching about a phenomenon that is on the decline. However, whether it is declining depends on how one defines "religion" and where in the world one looks! Evidence suggests that religion (howsoever it be defined) is thriving among the Global Majority and in regions the Global Majority calls home.[15] Data on migrants, refugees, and asylum seekers also points to the continued significance of religion, whether regarding their affiliation or the religious-based violence they are fleeing.[16] News stories remind us of the continued rise in antisemitism and Islamophobia not merely in North America but globally. Students should become educated in religious literacy to critically engage these complex issues. Some might concede this point, yet counter that religion's *influence* is on the decline! Theirs is a position difficult to support, since it is clear that religion remains a formative influence on political movements, electoral politics, and social policies in many parts of the world. Learning about religion in these contexts is a necessary step toward construction of meaningful responses. Given the "ambivalence of the sacred" (Scott Appleby's term), multireligious literacy enhances the ability to understand that religious traditions offer resources for both peace and violence, inclusion and exclusion, justice-seeking political activism and policies and positions that lead to injustice.[17] To those who argue that promotion of multireligious fluency should be left to religion-affiliated schools, the chapters in this volume demonstrate that more can be done. Still not swayed, someone asks, "Are we even *allowed* to teach religion in public schools?" The short answer is "Yes!" For a longer answer, see the Afterword.

# NOTES

1. See Christine J. Hong, *Decolonial Futures: Intercultural and Interreligious Intelligence for Theological Education* (Lanham, MD: Lexington Books, 2021). See also a review of Dr. Hong's book by Axel Takács in the *Journal of Interreligious Studies* 33 (August 2021):113–16. A succinct explanation of these terms is found in Axel Takács, "Critical Pedagogies in the Interfaith/Interreligious Studies Classroom: From the Editor-in-Chief," *Journal of Interreligious Studies* 36 (May 2022), 3–4.

2. See *Religion in the Public School Curriculum: Questions and Answers* (1988), cosigned by a number of organizations such as, including the American Academy of Religion, National School Board Boards Association, Association for Supervision and Curriculum Development, National Education Association, and religious educational organizations; National Council of Social Studies, *Including the study about religion in the social studies curriculum: A position statement and guidelines* (1990); and Association for Supervision and Curriculum Development, *Religious Liberty, Public Education, and the Future of American Democracy: A Statement of Principles* (1995).

3. Willam A. Nord and Charles C. Haynes, *Taking Religion Seriously Across the Curriculum* (Nashville, TN: First Amendment Center, 1998), 37.

4. See the work of Khyati Joshi, particularly *White Christian Privilege: The Illusion of Religious Equality in America* (New York: New York University Press, 2020).

5. S.G. Grant, John Lee, and Kathy Swan, "The State of the C3 Framework: An Inquiry Revolution in the Making," *Social Education* 87, no. 6 (Nov/Dec 2023): 362.

6. National Council for the Social Studies, *College, Career, and Civic Life (C3) Framework for Social Studies State Standards: Guidance for Enhancing the Rigor of K–12 Civics, Economics, Geography, and History* (Silver Spring, MD: NCSS), 2013, 6. Available online at https://www.socialstudies.org/standards/c3.

7. National Council for the Social Studies, *College, Career, and Civic Life (C3) Framework,* 92–97.

8. Benjamin Pietro Marcus, Kate Soules & David Callaway "National Summit on Religion and Education: A White Paper," *Religion & Education* 47, no. 1 (February 13, 2020): 2–18.

9. For the full text of *Journal of Interreligious Studies* 36 (May 23, 2022), see https://irstudies.org.

10. Khyati Joshi in *White Christian Privilege.*

11   See Lucinda Mosher, "What *Is* Interreligious Studies? Considerations from the 'Between'," in Lucinda Mosher, ed., *The Georgetown Companion to Interreligious Studies* (Washington, DC: Georgetown University Press, 2022), 3–14.

12   Katherine Janiec Jones and Cassie Meyer make this point in their essay, "Interfaith and Interreligious Pedagogies: An Assessment," in *Journal of Interreligious Studies* 36 (May 2022).

13   For short case studies of application across disciplines, the American Academy of Religion, *Guidelines for Teaching about Religion in K–12 Public Schools* (2010), Appendix D. Available online.

14   American Academy of Religion, *Guidelines*.

15   The term *Global Majority* in this case refers to non-white groups—specifically those of Indigenous, African, Asian, and Latin American descent—and to regions that, for the most part, correspond to the Global South. See Pew Research Center, "Key Findings From the Global Religious Futures Project," December 21, 2022.

16   See the Pew Research Center report, *Faith on the Move—the Religious Affiliation of International Migrants,* March 8, 2022. In addition, a survey of recent news stories reveals Christians fleeing violence in regions controlled by neo-Islamic fundamentalist groups, Rohingya Muslims fleeing violence in South Asia, Uighur Muslims fleeing violence in Xinjiang Province, China, Muslims under attack by Hindutva movements in India, and so much more.

17   R. Scott Appleby, *The Ambivalence of the Sacred: Religion, Violence, and Reconciliation* (Washington, DC: Rowman and Littlefield, 1999).

# Part I

# <u>Theory</u>

# 1

# EDUCATION ERADICATES IGNORANCE
## The Institute for Islamic, Christian, and Jewish Studies Teachers Fellowship

*Christine Gallagher*

"I usually just skip anything about religion because I don't want to make any students uncomfortable." As I sat and listened to a veteran teacher share this anecdote after I introduced myself at a national social studies educators' conference—in a session about a Supreme Court decision that very clearly dealt with the establishment and free exercise clauses—I couldn't help but think that maybe it was this teacher's own discomfort with religion that was driving his negligence toward his curriculum and students. And I was also grateful for the community of educators that I get to be a part of every year: teachers and administrators who are eager to dig into their curriculum, reflect on their own identities, and bring their learning back to their students.

For thirty-five years, the Institute for Islamic, Christian, and Jewish Studies (ICJS) has been convening learning communities across religious difference in the Baltimore area and beyond. We envision an interreligious society in which dialogue replaces division, friendship overcomes fear, and education eradicates ignorance.[1] We offer free public courses and online events. Our three fellowship programs—for educators, congregational leaders, and nonprofit/community leaders—create yearlong communities of study and networking. Now in its sixth year, our Teachers Fellowship cohorts discuss pivotal texts, learn with scholars, and share lesson plans and projects with each other. We challenge our educators to question the institutional, the curricular, the relational, and the personal.

I'm often asked for a single-page guide for teachers on "How to Teach About Religion." However, the reality is that there is no panacea for the complexities and questions stirred up by this work. Our fellowship gathers a devoted group of secondary school educators across institutions, subject matter, teaching experience, and religious identity in conversation with each other about religion, an identity and content matter often overlooked in schools. Educators come from public schools, independent schools, Jewish day schools, Muslim leadership schools, Episcopal schools, and Catholic schools. They teach social studies, world religions, Jewish studies, Catholic theology, English, ESOL, foreign languages, and even probability and statistics. They are also Diversity, Equity, Inclusion, and Belonging administrators, school chaplains, department chairs, and museum educators. They are early year teachers—fresh out of school or beginning their second career—and veteran educators, nearing retirement. They identify as Muslim, Christian, Jewish, and non-religious, with differing approaches to practice. Each of these identities inform the questions they ask and the conversations they have.

We begin our fellowship year by grounding our work in the interreligious: the blending and bleeding that happens in encounter and engagement. Some teachers—especially those in religious schools—are accustomed to a devotional or confessional approach; others are squarely in the religious studies camp. We invite them all to consider an interreligious framework in their teaching. How is their teaching about religion—whether it be a historical moment, a character in a piece of literature, a fact about our modern world—influenced by their own religious or non-religious identity, their students' religious or non-religious identities, the realities of how religion is talked about (and ignored) in the public square?

This is the first time that many of these teachers have had these discussions about religion. There are professional learning opportunities for many issues around school life—curriculum, identity, school culture—but few chances to discuss religion. There exists what I like to call a separation anxiety: many people believe that because of the so-called separation of church and state, it is unconstitutional to talk about religion in public schools. Baltimore is an important site in the history of these questions around religion and schools. In 1963, *Abington v. Schempp* consolidated the cases of a Pennsylvania school district and Baltimore City Public Schools. Both districts began school days with the recitation of the Lord's Prayer and a Bible passage, and Baltimore students could be excused by parental request. A Baltimore parent petitioned for the rule to be rescinded, citing a violation of the Establishment Clause. The district court and the Maryland Court of Appeals affirmed the rule. The Baltimore case was consolidated with the Pennsylvania case, and the Supreme Court ruled that the practice of Bible recitation and school prayer were unconstitutional.

But the court's ruling, written by Associate Justice Tom Clark, noted an important distinction when we talk about religion and schools:

> It might well be said that one's education is not complete without a study of comparative religion or the history of religion and its relationship to the advancement of civilization. It certainly may be said that the Bible is worthy of study for its literary and historic qualities. Nothing we have said here indicates that such study of the Bible or of religion, when presented objectively as part of a secular program of education, may not be affected consistently with the First Amendment.[2]

I tell teachers that they are part of a long line in the history of considering the importance of religious literacy and interreligious encounter in the classroom. I also point them toward the American Academy of Religion *Guidelines for Teaching About Religion in K-12 Public Schools in the United States* and the National Council for Social Studies *Religious Studies Companion Document for the C3 Framework*.

This fear of discussing religion and schools and the lack of professional development opportunities are what first drew me to ICJS. When I first arrived in Baltimore ten years ago, I was a world religions teacher in a Catholic school. I went to my principal to ask for help finding professional development opportunities. He pointed me toward ICJS, where I met secondary school teachers who had partnered with ICJS to create programming for other teachers. From its origins, ICJS teacher programming was teacher-led—secondary school educators who had experience in classrooms with teenagers were designing the programs in collaboration with ICJS scholars. But I also understand my privilege here: I was working in a religious school and assigned to teach about world religions. For many of my public school colleagues, a deeper fear existed. In the current educational climate, religious diversity is one of many hot topics, and many teachers are left wondering "if I teach about, say, Hinduism, or Islam, or Christianity, what will the reaction be? How many calls will I get from parents?" At ICJS, we want our teachers to come together and share those hesitancies and brainstorm together how to address them.

We have found that, because this type of professional learning is so new to some educators, we need to start with some basics. We use a short video to begin our discussion of religions and ground our thinking. The video, produced by Harvard Divinity School's Religion and Public Life program, states that religions are internally diverse, changing and evolving over time, and embedded in our lives and culture.[3] This is groundbreaking for many of our fellows. We assess how these ideas are present in their current work. From there, we look at two leading voices in the field: Diana Eck and Diane Moore.

Teacher fellows ponder Diana Eck's distinction between religious diversity and religious pluralism. They study her idea of "multivocality" and how we are bringing our different identities to different spaces.[4] Teachers consider what voice they use in the classroom versus at home versus in religious spaces. They reflect on a question that Eck raises: "What is a significant encounter you've had with someone who was religiously different from you, including non-religious people? What was significant about it?" In the process of responding, teacher fellows share their own experiences and encounters across difference; they also share their own orientations and biases toward religion. I often point to The Pluralism Project, which Eck founded, as a source for excellent resources and case studies in religion for their classrooms.

With Diane Moore, we return to questions of the classroom. Teacher fellows question their own assumptions in classroom settings and how to overcome them. Moore reminds us:

> ...the religious beliefs (or none) that educators hold will inevitably play themselves out in the classroom in conscious and unconscious ways. The aim is for educators to be as vigilantly aware as possible about their own assumptions while simultaneously interrogating their practices to minimize unconscious behaviors.[5]

Fellows interrogate their own experiences in their classrooms and institutions. They acknowledge that teaching about religion is not neutral; rather, it happens within national, local, and institutional contexts. This means different things for public school teachers than for teachers in religiously affiliated schools. They also acknowledge that they come to this work with different levels of knowledge of, and comfort with, talking about religion. We ask them what more they need to know.

It is in these moments of deep discussion—reflecting on teaching, uncovering biases, admitting knowledge gaps—that we get to know our teacher fellows; and we are constantly surprised! Our teachers show us the tough reality of religion in the public square. They also reveal the importance of asking questions of their curriculum and content.

- There's the public school teacher who often speaks up in equity discussions but never considered religion as part of the conversation and never thought about bringing her Jewish identity and voice into these spaces with her colleagues.

- There's the English teacher who comes to realize that religion is only a source of conflict in the stories her students read and wonders what it would mean for them to experience more nuanced portrayals of religion.

- There's the Catholic school teacher who has never taught a non-Catholic population and realizes that some of his students' discussions and jokes are really a reflection of anti-Jewish bias.

- There's the Muslim school teacher who speaks up in a lesson on the hajj with photos from her students' homemade recreation of that pilgrimage.

- There's the devout Christian public school teacher who hates teaching the Crusades because of the terrors that Christians wrought on Jewish and Muslim populations and struggles with what that means for her own religious expression.

- There's the new teacher in an overwhelmingly white and Christian public school district who's afraid that she really messed up when she tells a student that they can't focus on the Bible for a project about bestsellers.

All of these teachers spent a year in a learning community, bringing these questions to their peers.

Ignoring religion in the K-12 curriculum—in public, independent, or religious schools—simply perpetuates religious ignorance. However, if given the opportunity to engage in professional learning, teachers can overcome this ignorance and fear. As ICJS teachers expand their religious literacy and share curricular resources, they also engage in self-reflection. Together, they work to dialogue on difficult subjects, build friendship across difference, and educate themselves for the good of their students. This can be a model for the interreligious society.

## FOR REFLECTION

1  What anxieties arise for you when talking about religion in schools or with young people?

2  What assumptions and biases toward religion do you bring to this work?

3  Consider this question from Diana Eck: What is a significant encounter you've had with someone who was religiously different from you, including non-religious people? What was significant about it?

# NOTES

1. To learn more about the Institute for Islamic, Christian, and Jewish Studies and our work with teachers, see our website: www.icjs.org .

2. Abington v. Schempp, 374 U.S. 203 (1963).

3. "Misunderstandings About Religion" from *Religious Literacy: Traditions and Scriptures* (HarvardX), www.youtube.com.

4. Diana Eck, "Prospects for Pluralism: Voice and Vision in the Study of Religion," *Journal of the American Academy of Religion*, 75 (4): 770.

5. Diane Moore, *Overcoming Religious Illiteracy: A Cultural Studies Approach to the Study of Religion in Secondary Education* (New York: Palgrave Macmillan, 2007) 67.

# 2

# REIMAGINING RELIGION IN THE PUBLIC SCHOOL CLASSROOM

## A Close Look at a Pedagogical Shift

*John Camardella*

Conventional definitions of literacy often refer to a person's ability to read and write as a way to comprehend and interact with the world. These aptitudes are essential in preparing young adults for the world that awaits them upon graduation, but as we know, more is required these days. Educators and administrators across various educational contexts demand a lot from students in this rapidly changing world. Across the country, "literacy" courses in media technology, nutrition, and personal finance aim to assist students in navigating an ever-shifting landscape as conscientious adults. Generally, courses that promote learning to be responsible with digital devices, maintaining a healthy lifestyle, and managing money are highly valued among diverse communities. Although secondary schools regularly seek to enhance learning experiences across disciplines, agreement on one topic remains elusive and, when examined, highly contested: religion.

For those in the field, most realize that religion and its influences are present in all aspects of culture, yet there is a healthy tension in finding agreement on how best to approach the subject. Students need to be equipped with the language, knowledge, and skills to understand and engage in this diverse world, but serious questions remain. What is the best methodological approach to engaging religious theory and content in secondary schools?[1] How do course requirements and teacher constraints vary between public and private schools? What is at stake for this next generation, and how might this type of education vary based on geographical location? These questions, among others, have fueled my professional efforts. What follows is a short personal narrative of beginning a religious studies program and then pivoting mid-career to a new approach—the Cultural Studies Method—which I now see as the most effective and appropriate way for students to learn about religion.

## SITUATING THE NARRATIVE

I began teaching at Prospect High School outside of Chicago in 2003.[2] Although I have enjoyed teaching a variety of courses throughout my career, the past fifteen years of writing and developing my religion curriculum have been the greatest joy of my professional life. The idea came to me after an experience on the island of Bali in May of 2006, as I attended a global conference with the Archbishop of South Africa, Desmond Tutu. This gathering brought leaders together to increase understanding and improve religious literacy in personal, civic, and educational contexts.[3] As I returned home, I decided to commit myself to laying the groundwork for an elective religion course to be offered at my high school. Immediately that summer, I started emailing scholars of religion, interviewing faith leaders, and purchasing textbooks. However, as I began to write an initial curriculum, I soon realized there was no approved framework or set of national standards to guide educators like me. As a result, it took me years before the course was approved. The U.S. Supreme Court has upheld the right to teach about religion in public schools since 1963, when Justice Clark delivered the majority opinion in the Abington v. Schempp decision stating, "it might well be said that one's education is not complete without a study of comparative religion or the history of religion and its relationship to the advancement of civilization."[4] The most significant tension remains in the question of how educators should approach teaching the subject in secondary schools.

In the United States, most stand-alone religion courses use a textbook as a foundation. When I began in 2009, it was no different. My administration initially considered the textbook as the safest path—a way to protect ourselves from conflict and deliver basic content to students in a public school. For years, my lesson plans and assessments emphasized and essentialized content from different religious traditions, and student success was tied directly to their performance on multiple-choice exams. This Traditions-Based Approach privileges "certain categories that apply to many religious traditions, such as beliefs, texts, rituals, origins, and holidays" and often measures learning through standardized assessments.[5] As the years passed, my enrollment grew, and the curriculum remained unchanged. Students were learning, the response from parents was overwhelmingly positive, and the administration was happy. Why question the model or shift the approach?

## EXPANDING THE IMPACT & EXAMINING THE CURRICULUM

In 2015, I received an email from Benjamin Marcus, a religious literacy specialist, inviting me to meet with him and his team to discuss my work.[6] The two of us decided to collaborate on a handful of projects, and after co-hosting a religious studies conference at my high school in 2016, Marcus presented me with a new goal. He decided it was time to try to solve one of the most glaring deficiencies in this collective work: the lack of an approved set of guidelines for teaching about religion in secondary schools. Later that year, Marcus assembled a small writing team to produce a "Religious Studies" appendix to the National Council for Social Studies *Religious Studies Companion Document for the C3 Framework,* and I was honored to be one of two high school educators invited to contribute.[7] The National Council for the Social Studies publishes the *C3 Framework*, which was "developed to serve two purposes: for states to upgrade their state social studies standards and for practitioners—local school districts, schools, teachers, and curriculum writers—to strengthen their social studies programs."[8] The disciplines of Psychology, Sociology, and Anthropology all had their guidelines as part of the appendix, and our work focused on making sure religion would be taught in ways that are constitutionally sound and consistent with high academic standards. In the end, our *Religious Studies Companion Document* was endorsed by the American Academy of Religion and published by the National Council in June of 2017.

The NCSS press release explained that our document was "the product of a teacher-led initiative that launched at a conference for educators at Prospect High School in Mt. Prospect, IL [and] was developed by educators, school administrators, and subject matter experts from Harvard University and Rice University, with the support of the American Academy of Religion and of the Religious Freedom Center of the Newseum Institute."[9] Our introduction spoke to the civic duty secondary schools have in advancing this type of education as, "the study of religion from an academic, non-devotional perspective…is critical for decreasing religious illiteracy and the bigotry and prejudice it fuels."[10] Following the publication, Marcus shared how the achievement marked "the first time that a national education body has endorsed guidelines for how to teach religion from an academic standpoint."[11] This watershed moment also marked the time when I finally realized that my Traditions-Based curriculum had to change.

## A SHIFT IN TRAJECTORY

I first met Dr. Diane Moore of Harvard Divinity School during our work on the "Religious Studies Companion Document," as she framed the civic consequences of religious illiteracy in ways that forced me to reconsider my firmest convictions as an educator.[12] In all previous years, I had worked diligently to master the content needed to teach an effective religion course and believed sincerely that students benefited as a result. Thanks to Dr. Moore's influence, I recognized that the Traditions-Based Approach was not incorrect; it was just incomplete. The essentializing of content often reinforces problematic assumptions about the nature of religion.[13] To leave students ignorant of the internal diversity within religions is a great disservice and often leads to generalizations and stereotypes. As many people in the field acknowledge, a lack of understanding about how religion functions can lead to discrimination and violence and prevent cooperative endeavors across various contexts. The Traditions-Based Approach can also "exaggerate the commonalities among traditions [which are] often shaped by particular religious assumptions (including categories such as 'founder' and 'sacred text') that are not universally relevant and which therefore promote a biased and limited framework for analysis."[14] What I came to understand is that a more nuanced and complex understanding of religion, attained through the implementation of the Cultural Studies Method, can provide students with the necessary language and skills to discern how religion functions in a given social and historical context.

I believe the Cultural Studies Method to be a more sophisticated approach to studying religion in secondary schools as it can yield fresh insights on contemporary topics. More importantly, student engagement and learning occur at a deeper level, helping them become people able to address and transform their worlds in constructive ways. This approach places an "emphasis on recognizing the ways that religion is embedded in culture and cannot be understood in isolation from its particular social/historical expressions."[15] The Traditions-Based Approach leaves students unaware of internal diversity and reinforces the assumption that one religious interpretation or expression represents an entire tradition. By contrast, the Cultural Studies Method explains "that all knowledge claims are 'situated' in that they arise out of particular social/historical contexts and therefore represent particular rather than universally applicable claims."[16] Implementing this approach depends upon various forms of preparatory work to cultivate the necessary knowledge, concepts, and skills. Our course begins by having students confront the reality of "situatedness" by examining how they have come to understand their world as learners shaped by unique experiences.[17] As students prepare to address the situatedness of the content, they will recognize that a singular religious expression is an authentic but never an exclusive expression of a tradition.

## CULTURAL STUDIES IN ACTION

An average unit lasts roughly twenty days and includes a few introductory assignments that help students historically situate each religion. Before discussing any content, I am explicit that all concepts within a religious tradition are often contested and challenged in one way or another. Students learn how a specific term can take on a different meaning when understood in a different context, explore how diverse understandings develop, and consider what they might mean to those who order their lives on a specific interpretation. For this reason, any definitions or terms discussed in class are situated in a particular time and place and understood broadly as multifaceted. At the end of each unit, students no longer cram for lengthy exams filled with multiple-choice questions but instead investigate different themes through a case study model.[18] When I taught using the Traditions-Based Approach, students expected me to lecture, give them content to learn, and then assess them based on retention of information. I want to note that mastering religious concepts and vocabulary is a noble endeavor, but we can and must do more. Through the Cultural Studies Method, students build on the learned content by applying interpretive skills to engage and analyze a wide variety of contemporary religious expressions, political statements, and even legal decisions while envisioning a more just and peaceful world. In taking this extra step, students demonstrate their knowledge of religion— but with a deeper and richer understanding that manifestations are always culturally embedded, internally diverse, and evolving in complex and fascinating ways.

## CLASSROOM EXAMPLE: ENGAGING JEWISH TRADITIONS

Students will spend the first couple of days in our unit engaging with excerpts from the Hebrew Bible detailing the Law's revelation, learning some names and contributions, and contextualizing how Israel became the homeland of the Jewish people. Once complete, I can then provide a wide variety of primary and secondary resources for students to explore and analyze how Judaism is internally diverse, embedded in specific cultures, and has changed over time. For example, the class will explore a key figure, such as Maimonides, and then learn from various scholars how his writings and influence have impacted specific Jewish communities across cultures. For instance, there is considerable debate surrounding the use of fire and electricity on Shabbat, how one should observe Kaddish after the death of a loved one, and whether fasting is required on Yom Kippur. In these cases, offering voices from historical, religious, and secular perspectives will disrupt assumptions regarding how Judaism is practiced and provide scaffolding that encourages students to use proper vocabulary and rely on their critical thinking skills. Ultimately, this approach allows students to analyze authentic expressions throughout Judaism without accidentally conflating any single one with the religion as a whole.

## CLASSROOM EXAMPLE: ENGAGING HINDU TRADITIONS

To dive more deeply into addressing a sacred text, let's examine how we handle the ancient epic, the Ramayana. Students no longer read excerpts from this text as a single story with a single understanding but now consider how and why different versions of the Ramayana are told in other parts of India among diverse groups of Hindus. The class also considers contemporary depictions of scenes involving Rama, Sita, and Ravana in various comic books, television shows, or graphic novels that offer widely diverse portrayals. Students then explore the different ways the Ramayana is understood in the rise of contemporary Hindu Nationalism by using the language and skills of the Cultural Studies Method to analyze the various manifestations. Along the same lines, a subsequent reading of the Bhagavad Gita is also situated in a specific context, as students study its role in the life and teachings of Mahatma Gandhi.

## THE ROAD AHEAD

There is much at stake in improving this type of education for our next generation. Sadly, a lack of literacy in religious and cultural affairs has real-world consequences. Some of the most critical include a hindered ability to evaluate religious claims, a simplistic and shallow view of world events, and even a weakened capacity to critique the claims of those preaching religious intolerance and hate. To address this deficiency in my local community, I designed and launched an adult lecture series for the parents of our students in 2015. I wanted each family to have the opportunity to learn together, and each of the monthly sessions draws anywhere from forty to seventy participants. In my experience, most adults are only familiar with devotional approaches to religion, which are constitutionally inappropriate for our public school classroom. Our classes expose students to diverse religious views but never impose a particular perspective, and our parents learn this importance right away. Most importantly, it allows adults to witness how our curriculum features voices across religious and political spectrums and supports students' right to free exercise in engaging and analyzing various interpretations. If not addressed correctly, these tensions within communities can undermine the political will needed to support religious studies education in public schools. However, suppose educators and administrators are willing to honestly and respectfully engage parents regarding this educational moment. In that case, stakeholders can coalesce in support of the religious and cultural literacy work needed for themselves and their children.

For educators or administrators, adapting a curriculum or beginning a course with a Cultural Studies Approach is ambitious and will take a courageous commitment of many years to implement fully. Anyone involved in this work or preparing for a career in this field should expect pushback and challenges, but when approached correctly, I believe this work to be on the right side of history. Parker Palmer, an educator and author of multiple books on education, is succinct regarding the vital role an educator must play: "The teacher is a mediator between the knower and the known, between the learner and the subject to be learned. A teacher, not some theory, is the living link in the epistemological chain...and conveys both an approach to knowing and an approach to living."[19] This will always be formidable work, one worthy of our most profound efforts and steadfast dedication. Looking to the future, I see no greater calling than equipping young people with the knowledge and skills to interact confidently and engage respectfully with the beautifully diverse world we all experience and inhabit.

## FOR REFLECTION

1   Consider what a healthy and vibrant classroom community looks and feels like for students. How might using a Cultural Studies Approach enhance a learning environment?

2   Our understandings of the world are deeply rooted in personal experiences. Why is "situatedness" so critical to engaging and educating a diverse classroom of students?

3   Building a learning community is demanding, and often, progress is slow. How might the Cultural Studies Approach facilitate respectful dialogue between or among students?

# NOTES

1. For a more detailed analysis of the various approaches, see Diane L. Moore, et al, *American Academy of Religion Guidelines for Teaching About Religion in K–12 Public Schools in the United States* (Atlanta, GA: The American Academy of Religion, 2010), 9–10.

2. Prospect High School is located in Mount Prospect, Illinois and is part of High School District 214.

3. The Quest for Global Healing II was organized by the Bali Institute. The conference was held in the city of Ubud on the island of Bali, Indonesia in May 2006.

4. Tom Campbell Clark and Supreme Court of The United States. U.S. Reports: Abington School District v. Schempp, 374 U.S. 203 (1962). Periodical. https://www.loc.gov/item/usrep374203.

5. Moore, *AAR Guidelines*, 10.

6. Tom Campbell Clark and Supreme Court.

7. The writing team was composed of the following individuals (in alphabetical order): Jessica Blitzer, West Hartford Public Schools (CT); Seth Brady, Naperville Central High School (IL); John Camardella, Prospect High School (IL); Niki Clements, Rice University (TX); Susan Douglass, Georgetown University (DC); Benjamin P. Marcus, Newseum Institute (DC); Diane L. Moore, Harvard Divinity School (MA); and Nathan C. Walker, Teachers College Columbia University (NY).

8. National Council for the Social Studies (NCSS), *The College, Career, and Civic Life (C3) Framework for Social Studies State Standards: Guidance for Enhancing the Rigor of K–12 Civics, Economics, Geography, and History*, (Silver Spring, MD, 2013).

9. "Academic Study of Religion Added to Social Studies Guidelines," https://www.socialstudies.org. June 2017.

10 . "College, Career & Civic Life C3 Framework," *C3 Framework for Social Studies*, (National Council for the Social Studies, June 2017), 93. See https://www.socialstudies.org.

11. Diane Rado, "National Education Group Recommends Religious Studies in K–12 Public Schools," *Chicago Tribune*, June 4, 2018.

12. For a comprehensive overview of Cultural Studies, see: Diane L. Moore, *Overcoming Religious Illiteracy: A Cultural Studies Approach to the Study of Religion in Secondary Education*. (New York: Palgrave Macmillan, 2007).

13. Such content can be doctrines, ethics, sacred texts, rituals, founders, symbols, and so on.

14. Moore, *AAR Guidelines*, 10.

15. Moore, *AAR Guidelines*, 10.

16. Diane L. Moore, "Overcoming Religious Illiteracy."

17. For an elaboration of situatedness see: Donna Haraway, "Situated Knowledges: The Science Question in Feminism and the Privilege of Partial Perspective" in *Simians, Cyborgs, and Women: The Reinvention of Nature* (New York: Routledge, 1991).

18. For a detailed account of my shift from standardized assessments to a case study model, see: Caroline Matas, "Religious education through new eyes," *The Harvard Gazette* (July 30, 2018).

19. Parker J. Palmer, *To Know as We Are Known: Education as a Spiritual Journey* (San Francisco: Harper San Francisco, 1983), 29.

# 3
# DECOLONIZING RELIGIOUS EDUCATION IN INTERNATIONAL SCHOOLS
## Curriculum Redesign Toward Religious Literacy

*Renee L. Bowling*

Historically religiously affiliated international schools have seen significant changes to their student bodies and staff makeup. While many of these institutions were founded at the height of colonialism as Christian missionary schools, the student populations of these schools are increasingly marked by diversity, including religious pluralism. Staff have diversified and professionalized, having been drawn from many of the same recruitment pools as secular international schools and teaching common curricula, often with an added religious education component. As a foreign staff member in one such school in Asia, I was sensitive to the historical context and troubled by the colonial approach to religious education students encountered. This birthed questions about what postcolonial religious education looks like around the world and how it might intersect with the educational mission of contemporary international schools. Pursuit of these questions and a desire to honor both my school's heritage and students' religious pluralism led to my facilitation of a collaborative redesign of the school's religious education curriculum to one of religious literacy. This is the story of one educator's journey in one international school and lessons learned as we collectively consider how to decolonize religious education.

## THE CONTEXT

The K–12 international school that inspired this journey was situated in a diverse region of Asia with Hindu, Buddhist, Muslim, Christian, Sikh, Jewish, Parsi, and indigenous religions represented in the student body. The school was founded by Americans in the 1850s as an interdenominational missionary project for the private education of expatriate girls and local students. Over time, it became co-educational, with increasing diversity. Prompted by the nation's postcolonial visa policies, the school transitioned from primarily mission-funded Christian expatriate faculty to a religiously plural professional teaching staff in the late twentieth century and from a missionary school to a Christian international school identity. The colonial tradition of Christian education continues to enjoy a strong reputation in the region and the school is recognized as a leading international school.

The school's self-perpetuating governing board includes reserved seats for Protestant Christian denominations connected to the school's history. It is charged with upholding the Christian character of the school, which it enacts through appointment of the principal and chaplain and endorsement of the school's religious life policy. This policy underscores the school's Christian heritage and acknowledges religious pluralism, differentiating between chaplaincy and compulsory religious education, which are both intended to be "inclusively Christian." In addition to a full-time chaplain, a teacher serves a supplemental assignment as Religious Education coordinator responsible for the Religious Education curriculum. Christianity is firmly centered in both chaplaincy and Religious Education, although other religious backgrounds and identities are welcomed and celebrated.

## POSITIONALITY AS KEY

I joined the school as the faculty was becoming more religiously diverse and as the chaplains were increasingly emphasizing the inclusive aspect of Christianity. The makeup of the student body had long since shifted to reflect the national composition, placing minoritized Christian students in the paradoxical position of encountering both institutional privilege and derision from their peers. I served as a school counselor and teacher and volunteered with Religious Education retreats, eventually moving into roles as a head of department and head of secondary.

My positionality is key to understanding my journey as an instructional leader of Religious Education. I entered the history of the school as a white American Christian faculty member. My whiteness, affiliation with evangelical Christianity, faculty status, and nationality afforded me privilege and access to the Religious Education program. My Christianity in particular gave me insider status to influential local and expat Christian communities. On the other hand, my multicultural family and faith practice aligned me with religiously different neighbors who, like the student body, reflected the majority religious communities of the country. This combined emic/etic perspective enabled me to observe how Christianity can function with privilege in international schools despite Christian communities being minoritized in the national context. In postcolonial spaces where parent and community members have internalized colonial beliefs about the superiority of Western education and view access to the school as instrumental to Western opportunities, Christian and White privilege can reinforce one another and perpetuate coloniality.

I observed that students of varied religious, secular, and spiritual communities resented the imposition of Christianity in their daily lives and academics. The school presented an odd mixture of both structural privilege and individual discrimination for the Christian student minority from their peers, while the students of other identities had to navigate the structural privilege of normative Christianity, compulsory Christian chapels, Christianity-centered Religious Education, and bias against their own worldviews from some of the faculty.[1]

## THE INHERITED RELIGIOUS EDUCATION CURRICULUM

Religious Education consisted of weekly compulsory classes at all levels, taught from a Christian perspective by Christian teachers. Although theoretically aligned with the school's learning outcomes of knowledge of self and others and intercultural competence, neither were assessed formally. Elementary education focused on Bible stories; the middle school curriculum introduced other traditions, always alongside Christianity. Ninth graders took an introduction to Christianity course and tenth graders, a survey of world religions, followed by philosophy and ethics electives in grades 11–12.

While proselytizing teachers had become a matter of alumni lore, the inherited Religious Education curriculum fell far short of actual inclusion. It institutionalized Christian hegemony by prioritizing Christianity in course topics, teaching time, and teacher assignments, and by ensuring that other religions were taught from a Christian comparative perspective. As an example, the world religions course was framed as phenomenological but was grounded in Western assumptions of religions as textual and focused on eschatological and soteriological questions. The first half of the year was dedicated to Judeo-Christian traditions despite these being minoritized in the community. Students dutifully learned content but remained suspicious of the latent purpose of Religious Education.

During my tenure, the school embarked on a wholesale curriculum change, adopting the International Baccalaureate in grades 5–12. As a member of the accreditation team, I was deeply aware of the gap between the inquiry basis of the curriculum the school was about to adopt and the aims and pedagogies of the Religious Education program. It was a vestige of the past: teacher-centered, focused on didactic methods and facts about static religions from a Western perspective that too often placed students in the position of spokespersons for diverse traditions. The impending departure of the Religious Education coordinator and the school's transition to a new curriculum meant that the subject of Religious Education could easily have been lost in the shuffle. Yet this also presented an opportunity for curricular review and innovation.

I had been an observer of Religious Education for some time, pondering what a postcolonial version could look like. As a U.S. citizen, I was aware of the poor state of religious literacy and engagement with religious difference in public education in my own country. The context of the school was highly pluralistic and had a history of intergroup conflict in which religion was enmeshed with culture, identity, and politics. Clearly, ignoring religious difference would not do, and the existing approach was doing little to foster interreligious curiosity or understanding. This is when I began looking externally to seek postcolonial approaches to religious education and became interested in intersections between Religious Education and the educational mission of contemporary international schools.

## Seeking and Finding: A Collaborative Redesign

Scanning the international school landscape, I found two main approaches to Religious Education. Many religiously-affiliated schools were using their own curricula passed down over the years much as my school was, while others adopted a syllabus that had been imported from a Religious Education teacher's country of origin. The most frequent delivery method was to tack a Religious Education requirement on top of an international curriculum. In most cases, Religious Education continued to be taught with methods in direct contrast to the inquiry expected in other subjects. Rather than opening up possibilities to explore spiritual ways of knowing and connections to other subjects, the message students were receiving was to question everything, but not in Religious Education class.

This led me to study approaches from other countries and to connect with Harvard's Religious Literacy Project, which has since been folded into its Religion and Public Life initiative.[2] This exposed me to an array of pedagogical approaches to teaching religious literacy. I consequently pursued further study in religious studies and education that introduced me to the tenets of a cultural studies approach.[3] I appreciated its emphases on the impossibility of neutrality in education and Freireian pedagogy. I eventually incorporated these into teaching my school's world religions course, which served as an experimental ground for a larger curriculum redesign.

I secured permission to take on Religious Education coordination in addition to my other duties, assembling a core team to collaboratively redesign Religious Education and make recommendations for how it might function with the new curriculum. The other core team members were the chaplain and the International Baccalaureate Middle Years Program Coordinator (an Individuals and Societies teacher). The team was selected for our interest in the project, our backgrounds with religious education, familiarity with the International Baccalaureate, and openness to innovation. Regrettably, all core team members were White expats of secular and/or Christian backgrounds; this was a serious compositional flaw. During the academic year leading up to the International Baccalaureate curriculum implementation, we worked together to define the aims of the school's Religious Education curriculum. Shortly following this work, the governing board expressed concern for the continuance of Religious Education. An external consultant from the U.K.'s Religious Education Council was folded into our process and ultimately endorsed it.

The key challenges the team sought to address were structural, content-based, and pedagogical. Structurally, we had decisions to make: whether to work within the existing learning outcomes or the International Baccalaureate's; whether to require Religious Education as a standalone subject; and, if required, who would teach it—and how this would work with new teaching loads. We determined that other decisions should follow first principles. Therefore, we set about establishing the following Religious Education Aims for our school, drawing from the religious literacy competencies endorsed by the American Academy of Religion:[4]

- Identify differing understandings of the nature and perception of truth and of human relationships to the divine/ultimate

- Distinguish between the academic study of religion and spiritual/devotional practice

- Explore the context of beliefs and the role of faith

- Develop an informed understanding of the internal diversity of religions

- Recognize religion's embeddedness in and impact on culture, history, and society

- Understand religion as dynamic, changing with time, place, and space

In a concise document, the core team demonstrated the Religious Education Aims' connection to the school's learning outcomes and International Baccalaureate subject goals. Incorporation of the Aims was ultimately more important than recalling facts, which guided our content work. We sought to honor the religious life policy of exposure to Christianity and to the diverse religions represented in our community in a way that would be accessible and inclusive, giving teachers freedom to choose texts and examples.

The core team members agreed that the same spirit of inquiry found in the learning outcomes should guide the pedagogical approach. Our emphasis on skills over content implied that teaching was accessible through training and did not rely on specialized content knowledge. This represented a significant shift, opening up the teaching of Religious Education beyond dedicated Christian faculty. Surveying the options for Religious Education as a standalone subject, we realized that extending the day beyond required International Baccalaureate subjects would burden students already adapting to a rigorous curriculum and would require additional staff to execute. Alternatively, there existed potential for curricular infusion given the compatibility of skills-based learning with the International Baccalaureate. The core team explored possible International Baccalaureate subject area connections and identified the social studies subject Individuals and Societies as the best fit for grades 5–10.[5] We determined that homeroom teachers could continue to teach Religious Education in the early years, and that grades 11–12 could encounter philosophical themes within the International Baccalaureate Theory of Knowledge course if designed attentive to our Religious Education Aims. It should be noted this was prior to the International Baccalaureate Organization's revision of the Theory of Knowledge course. At the time, religious knowledge systems and ethics were "areas of knowledge" and faith was one of the "ways of knowing" schools could elect to include in their syllabi. We intentionally included these to foster our students' engagement with spiritual and indigenous epistemologies. The largest task for curriculum infusion work, therefore, was in the middle years' Individuals and Societies units.

At this stage, we involved the elementary head, the Individuals and Societies department head, and the Theory of Knowledge lead teacher in planning, followed by these subjects' K–12 teachers who represented multiple religious identities and nationalities. We provided training on the Religious Education Aims with activities to support their interpretation in different grade levels. Training included selection of resources and assessment design screened through the lens of the Religious Education Aims, how to conduct inquiry-based lessons with the teacher serving as a facilitator, and how to reframe student generalizations to become teachable moments. The team mapped out two units per year across grades 5–10 that met Individuals and Societies objectives and embedded parallel Religious Education Aims in unit plans.

Because they were treated as curricular experts, teachers felt a sense of ownership, so were instrumental in the creation of the new units. I consulted similarly with elementary teachers over the next academic year to help them devise a two-year rotation of Religious Education units for their multi-grade homerooms (for example,  Gr. 1–2, Gr. 3–4). The core team's role was to check for breadth of religious traditions, representation of texts and praxis, inclusion of Religious Education Aims horizontally and vertically, and to ensure that the units included Christian themes and stories throughout the curriculum, congruent with the religious life policy. In practice, the redesign resulted in a decentering of Christianity in the Religious Education program's delivery while still ensuring exposure to Christianity throughout all levels.

Finally, we collaborated with individual teachers on their International Baccalaureate unit planning to help them think through their resource needs, artifacts, and assessments aligned with both Religious Education and International Baccalaureate objectives. Unit planning took place the semester prior to implementation with professional development and coaching available throughout the first year.

The resulting elementary units focused on students' family backgrounds and thematic exposure to the top three religions represented in the school community, such as through a unit on festivals. The middle years incorporated perspectives on human nature, wisdom, the divine, and morality and exposed students to literature including the Bhagavad Gita, the Qur'an, the Pentateuch, New Testament, and Jataka Tales. An example unit on significant individuals involved figures from three different traditions and their key teachings studied in historical, geographical, and social context. In grades 9–10, a two-year Integrated Humanities course was planned to culminate in an external exam assessing economics, geography, and world history skills. The team chose to incorporate the Religious Education Aims and Religious Education-themed content throughout all of the grade 9 units, embedded in Individuals and Societies defined "global contexts" of identities and relationships, orientation in space and time, personal and cultural expression, and fairness and development. This particular curriculum work led to rich Religious Education-infused units on identity, displacement and diffusion, peace and conflict, and poverty and inequality. Importantly, the curriculum modeled the Religious Education Aims by incorporating the role of faith embodied in both belief and practice in diverse ways, representing religions as dynamic and embedded in culture, society, and history, impacting specific places and times.

## LESSONS LEARNED

Since the redesign I have had the opportunity for further study of decolonizing curriculum and pedagogies, and I am convinced of the importance of such work being contextual and locally determined. Hindsight reveals both strengths and weaknesses to our work. I apply observed decolonizing curriculum and pedagogy practices from Shahjahan and others to unpack the lessons learned from this particular project.[6]

### CRITIQUING THE POSITIONALITY OF KNOWLEDGE

This project intentionally shifted the location of knowledge from an external authority to a community-based authority that explored multiple epistemologies and involved teachers and students in the co-creation of knowledge. The project sought to keep a Christian thread throughout the curriculum while weaving with it threads of other religious traditions. As Shahjahan and others would put it, we "prioritized community knowledge over institutional legitimacy."[7] By taking a thematic approach to unit planning, the redesign decentered Christianity to be one among many, not the standard by which other religions were measured. By emphasizing the internal diversity and contextuality of religions the internal diversity of Christianity itself was expanded.

### CONSTRUCTING INCLUSIVE CURRICULUM

The decision to honor and work within the school's religious life policy enabled significant reform to take place. The timing of other changes in the school mattered, creating possibility which the core team took advantage of to identify first principles and allow these to guide the redesign. The team leaned on the inclusivity present in the school's policy, intentionally sought to equitably represent the diversity of religions present, and involved teachers of multiple religious identities in the creation of the units. However, the redesign could have been much more inclusive of students and the religious communities represented in the school. Stakeholders, including students and parents, could have been included through surveys or focus groups, and a greater diversity of religions should have been represented in the core team, not just the teaching team.

### COLLABORATIVELY PRODUCING KNOWLEDGE THROUGH RELATIONAL APPROACHES

The Religious Education Aims implied a learner-centered pedagogy that was able to be conveyed successfully in teacher trainings. Once teachers understood they were not expected to be Religious Education subject matter experts, it opened new possibilities to shift the student-teacher relationship and explore religious and spiritual knowledge. The cultural studies approach in particular gives teachers tools to discuss lived religion rather than treating religions as static or disconnected from the lives and actions of individuals and societies. The focus on skills over content and infusion with social studies topics helps enable these connections in the classroom.

## Connected to Community and Sociopolitics

This project centered the religious communities represented in the region and particular school community, shifting the Religious Education program from Christian among others; from the earliest ages, it also prioritized the students' own experience of the world and their community. While the Religious Education Aims ensure connection to communities and sociopolitics through their emphases on internal diversity, context, culture, and change, the redesign could have gone further to explicitly encourage self-reflexivity and explore privilege and power. While self-reflexivity was an aspect of teacher training, power and privilege are included in units as a result of the "Individuals and Societies" themes and global contexts included in the International Baccalaureate's Middle Years Programme more than Religious Education Aims themselves. A curricular revision that seeks to be decolonizing from the outset might connect with and prioritize critical religious studies perspectives.

The core team's engagement with power could also have been more strategic. While we were conscious of the governing board's power and the need to conform to policy, we chose to operate under the authority of school administrators. Had the board been cultivated all along, their endorsement may have led to greater sustainability of the new Religious Education program. Through unrelated circumstances, the school encountered a high degree of turnover two years later leading to a great deal of institutional knowledge loss. While curriculum maps and unit plans exist, they are of little practical use if there is no one who remembers where to access them.

At the time, both the external consultant and Religious Education core team argued for the importance of a Religious Education coordinator to ensure sustainability of the Religious Education program. We foresaw the danger of having no one ultimately responsible for training teachers or assessing outcomes. I remain convinced formal oversight is critical to an infusion model's success. Faculty have their own subject outcomes to concern themselves with, and the isomorphic pressures of external curriculum review and accreditation processes do not prioritize Religious Education as an area of instruction. If a school wishes to make the subject a priority, it should designate a coordinator and budget, formalize dotted lines to infused subjects, and require reporting on Religious Education learning outcomes.

Established curricula have a way to go to include religion and spirituality into their ecology of knowledges.[8] Until then, independent schools with inherited religious education curricula have choices about how they approach Religious Education and to what extent those approaches contribute to recolonizing or decolonizing the subject. I encourage practitioners to learn from our project's missteps, to keep learning about decolonizing curriculum and pedagogy, and to connect with like-minded practitioners as they consider the possibilities for their unique contexts.

## For Reflection

1   Of the features identified in this story, which are most salient to your context: positionality, context and history, structural elements, or impetus for change?

2   What are some of the constraints and opportunities faced by religiously-affiliated teachers in non-sectarian independent schools who seek to decolonize religious education?

3   How do the stated goals of your religious education program connect to the school's larger educational philosophy and pedagogy? Are they compatible or do they conflict? What assumptions are embedded in your current approach?

# NOTES

1. K. Y. Joshi, *White Christian Privilege: The Illusion of Religious Equality in America* (New York, NY: New York University Press, 2020).

2. Diane L. Moore, "Methodological Assumptions and Analytical Frameworks Regarding Religion," https://hds.harvard.edu/files/hds/files/religious-literacy-project-method.pdf.

3. Diane L. Moore, *Overcoming Religious Illiteracy: A Cultural Studies Approach to the Study of Religion in Secondary Education* (New York, NY: Palgrave Macmillan, 2007).

4. American Academy of Religion. *AAR Religious Literacy Guidelines*, aarweb.org.

5. International Baccalaureate Individuals and Societies Middle Years Programme subject aims from school's internal documents:

- appreciate human and environmental commonalities and diversity
- understand the interactions and interdependence of individuals, societies and the environment
- understand how both environmental and human systems operate and evolve
- identify and develop concern for the well-being of human communities and the natural environment
- act as responsible citizens of local and global communities
- develop inquiry skills that lead towards conceptual understandings of the relationships between individuals, societies and the environments in which they live.

6. Riyad A. Shahjahan, Annabelle L. Estera, Kristen L. Surla, and Kirsten T. Edwards. "'Decolonizing' Curriculum and Pedagogy: A Comparative Review Across Disciplines and Global Higher Education Contexts." *Review of Educational Research* (2021).

7. Shahjahan et al., "Decolonizing Curriculum and Pedagogy," 15.

8. Boaventurra de Sousa Santos, "Beyond abyssal thinking: From global lines to ecologies of knowledges," *Review* (Fernand Braudel Center) 30, no. 1 (2007): 45–89.

# 4

# TOWARD GREATER APPRECIATION

## Religious Literacy in K–12 Education

*Christopher Murray*

Schools and classrooms in the United States are increasingly religiously diverse, and religion remains a deeply influential social force, locally, nationally, and globally. However, decades of misunderstanding about the constitutionally appropriate relationship between religion and public education have created a cycle of silence about religion in K–12 schools and in teacher education. As a result, public school educators are not prepared to include religion in the curriculum; nor do they have the skills to respond to common challenges that arise in religiously diverse school communities. According to research by Kate E. Soules, educators working at all grade levels and in all content areas garner valuable benefits from increasing their understanding of religion, including a greater appreciation for the religious identities of their students and increased comfort with religion when it appeared in a range of school settings.[1]

Religious literacy requires both a familiarity with the key vocabulary of multiple religious languages, (for example, knowing the names of various holy books) while also grappling with the many ways individuals and communities construct their religious identities through shared beliefs, ritual behaviors, and the experiences of belonging to a community—festivals, for example. Effective communication with the religious other depends on utilizing a similar grammar and referencing shared aspects of religious identity as much as, if not more than, using the same vocabulary. As educators, we want to move past the simple graphic organizer of world religions and explore the ways billions of people today live their religions.

Having a deep understanding of students' backgrounds and identities is essential for teachers to develop strong relationships with their students. However, the discussion or acknowledgment of religious identity is largely avoided in teacher education programs, in professional development offerings, and in the classroom. Passively ignoring, or actively avoiding, students' religious identities can have harmful effects on students' experiences in school and hinder the development of positive relationships with teachers and staff. A common theme in both the interviews and survey conducted in Soules' research was that increased knowledge about religions helped teachers to understand their students more and improved their relationships with them.

For example, a high proportion of students who are members of minoritized religions experience bullying, discrimination, and misunderstanding in schools. A religion-based version of "colorblindness" may lead teachers to think the bullying is *not* directed at the student's religion but at something else.[2] Increased knowledge about religion enabled educators to recognize religious identities and understand how students might want, or not want, those identities to be acknowledged in the classroom. This led educators to be more comfortable talking to students about religion and asking students questions about their religions.

Being familiar with the language for talking about religion is an important step in becoming more comfortable discussing and teaching about religion. Recent research has found that the use of language about religion and spirituality has declined in everyday conversation and in written works.[3] Without some knowledge about religion and comfort with the language and vocabulary—the building blocks of literacy—it will be challenging to increase understanding about religious diversity. Educators who can take a course in religious literacy will develop a vocabulary of lived religion and the confidence to bring those conversations into their schools and classrooms. When teachers are not provided with appropriate education about religion, they are likely to fall back on the stereotypes and impressions that they have picked up from popular media, their family and cultural backgrounds, or even lessons from childhood religious education, such as Sunday school. It is critical that educators acknowledge the realities and power of religion in the world so that they can help to form students as citizens who have the knowledge, skills, and dispositions to engage with religious pluralism in their communities and around the world.

For an example, we can look to Maryland's Montgomery County Public Schools. Since the summer of 2016, this district has offered a three-credit professional development course entitled Religious Literacy for Educators. To date, this course has been offered eleven times, thus has educated more than 350 faculty and staff within the school system. Additionally, the course was the catalyst for a 2017 Association fo Supervision and Curriculum Development Teacher Impact Grant in partnership with the US Department of Education that provided funding for two school districts in the Chicagoland area to create similar summer courses. The validity of courses like Religious Literacy for Educators was the subject of Soules' dissertation mentioned above, which produced strong evidence of the value of such a course.[4] Additionally, the summer 2019 cohort received a favorable write-up in the *Washington Post*.[5]

The inspiration for launching the course came from the 2015 school board decision to remove all religious holiday designations from the 2016 calendar. While the decision to remove religious holidays was clearly an appropriate decision in First Amendment terms, it failed to address the calls from members of the community who had hoped the school system would not have class instruction on Eid al-Fitr, Diwali, and Lunar New Year. Additionally, other news outlets covered this decision as part of their "War on Christmas" coverage. I was fortunate enough to have been a part of the first cohort of a program on religion and the First Amendment created by Nate Walker at the Religious Freedom Center.[6] I felt I could help my fellow educators make the most of this opportunity. I got the full support of our school superintendent, who asked the Maryland State Department of Education to approve the professional development course. With the support of my union, Montgomery County Education Association, I was successful in getting the course approved for a five-year run. I went about partnering with local religious leaders and scholars to craft the most meaningful way to spend forty-five hours exploring religion in our community. Over the years, I have adapted the course to meet the growing needs of the county, including addressing rises in hate crimes against East Asian Americans and better understanding Evangelicalism in America generally and the Latin America community particularly.

Before the Covid-19 pandemic, we spent the classes exploring local houses of worship, often speaking with current students in our school systems about what their religions mean to them and ways in which we can better support our students. We tackled tough topics like xenophobia and dove deeper into other forms of discrimination that we find in our schools, like transphobia and the intersection religion can play. We worked with the White House, the Department of State, and the US Institute of Peace. We were able to shift the 15-week program online during the pandemic. This gave us access a far greater array of experts from around the country who would spend forty minutes lecturing on their research before engaging in a Q&A with educators on ways they can better serve their students and their families of various religious traditions.

The feedback has been wonderful to hear from all parties involved, from federal government officials who praise Montgomery County Public Schools [MCPS] for being a leader in religious literacy training, to community members who feel safer knowing more teachers understand who their children are in school. However, the greatest feedback has been from teachers who rose to the challenge of an intense and tiring course that in the matter of one week took them all over the area and exposed them to so many deep topics. Here is what three of them had to say:[7]

> I am impressed and grateful to have been a part of the experience. It was an enriching and valuable experience for all educators, especially social studies teachers. MCPS went above and beyond to plan, facilitate, and lead the course. From what I've seen, heard, and read, the course experiences were also a product of MCPS participation in a range of community experiences and partnerships all in the name of educating students and teachers.
>
> – *Chris Ascienzo*
> *Social Studies Content Specialist*
> *Farquhar Middle School*

> The speakers MCPS got for us were incredible and I can't tell you how lucky I feel to have been able to be a part of this and to have met such amazing people. I appreciate the effort MCPS put into making this class so phenomenal....I have grown not only intellectually this week, but emotionally and spiritually as well. I have already been researching religions more on my own since the class ended and cannot wait to impart some of my newfound knowledge to my students. Thank you for such a rich, fulfilling experience!
>
> – *Kimberly Maffeo*
> *Spanish Teacher*
> *Sligo Creek Middle School*

> I participated in this class, and the information helps me make a more inclusive class for my students. I am more attentive to possible bullying because a student might not shave her body hair, {might] follow a vegan diet, [or] wear ashes on their forehead, or fast all day long during Ramadan.  The class is more about understanding other people than promulgating religion.
>
> – *Alberto Butternut*

I fully recognize that, in today's climate, not every teacher is as fortunate as I am to be able to teach freely about religions and to lead training on religious literacy.

The good news is that the First Amendment can support teachers and schools as they become empowered to tackle religious illiteracy in the classroom. Amazing experts and advocates who have decades of experience working with schools and fighting for teachers are just a phone call or email away. I encourage everyone to explore the many organizations with First Amendment-friendly resources and lesson plans. The community of religious literacy advocates continues to grow each year and we are always excited and willing to help educators join the movement.

## FOR REFLECTION

1   In the classroom, what are ways you can show and explore how people normalize the wide varieties of religious traditions and practices that so many of our students hold near and dear to themselves?

2   At a school level, what can be done to combat religious illiteracy and bullying of students of various religious and non-religious traditions?

3   At a district level, what can educators do to reach out and make meaningful connections with religious communities in your school district and provide a way for them to share concerns?

# NOTES

1.  Kate E. Soules, "The Impact of Professional Development on Public School Teachers' Understanding of Religious Diversity." Doctoral Dissertation, Boston College, 2019.

2.  Murali Balaji, Raman Khanna, Aditi Dinakar, Harsh Voruganti, and Kavita Pallod, "Classroom Subjected Bullying and Bias Against Hindu Students in American Schools," (Hindu American Foundation 2016), www.hafsite.org.

3.  See, for example: Barna Group, Gen Z: Your Questions Answered (February 6, 2018), barna. com; P. Kesebir and S. Kesebir, "The cultural salience of moral character and virtue declined in twentieth century America," *The Journal of Positive Psychology 7*, no. 6 (2012): 471–80.

4.  Kate E. Soules, "The Impact of Professional Development."

5.  Julie Weil Zauzmer, "Religion in school can be complicated. So teachers went to class," *Washington Post* (July 5, 2019), www.washingtonpost.com.

6. Sadly, that program is no longer offered.

7. These teachers have given permission for their comments to be shared here with attribution.

# 5
# RELIGIONS IN SOCIAL STUDIES CLASSROOMS
## Three Perspectives

*John Shekitka*

When I look at the ways that religions are discussed as part of the curriculum in the field of secondary social studies education in the United States of America, three broad approaches emerge: 1) understanding religions as cultural systems; 2) understanding religions as *sui generis* phenomena; and 3) critiques of "religion" and "religions" as coherent conceptual categories altogether. I hope that reviewing and categorizing the literature from this field's past two decades will help in unpacking and addressing some of the challenges in teaching about religions in classrooms in a variety of secondary school settings. Ultimately, I argue that teachers should be more intentional in theorizing the concept of "religions" with their secondary students. In what ways are religions a part of culture and in which ways are they unique? Further, teachers and students alike would be best served in understanding and discussing how the category "religion" and how we demarcate one religion from another are products of the post-Enlightenment West. Such a move is consistent with broader trends in secondary social studies education. That is, students are to be critics of the disciplines of religious studies and interreligious studies themselves, much in the same way they are asked to unpack the notions of "history" and "civics" and interrogate their underlying meaning, constructedness, and historical evolution.[1]

## UNDERSTANDING RELIGIONS AS CULTURAL SYSTEMS

Is religion simply culture by another name? Many scholars of religious studies, particularly those rooted in the field of anthropology, contend that there is a broad overlap between religion and culture.[2] According to Emile Durkheim, "a religion is a unified system of beliefs and practice relative to sacred things, that is to say, things set apart and forbidden—beliefs and practices which unite into one single moral community called a Church, all those who adhere to them."[3] The word "Church" notwithstanding, Durkheim's definition could likely allow one to define most cultural systems as religions—be they organized on ethnic, nationalistic, or other ideological bases. It would not be too much of a stretch to argue that the US, or any other purportedly secular nation-state, is a religion based on Durkheim's definition.[4] Clifford Geertz, who built upon the anthropological religious studies work of Durkheim, defines religion in a very similar anthropological way. According to Geertz,

> A *religion* is: (1) a system of symbols which acts to (2) establish powerful, pervasive, and long-lasting moods and motivations in men by (3) formulating conceptions of a general order of existence and (4) clothing these conceptions with such an aura of factuality that (5) the moods and motivations seem so uniquely realistic.[5]

Consequently, taking an anthropological view of religion, one finds that justifying the study of religions as part of social studies is in many ways analogous to justifying the study of cultures.

While not rooted explicitly in the anthropology of religion, a large body of literature clearly sees religion as a phenomenon that is closely analogous to culture. Many of these studies suggest that an increase in the study of religions leads to increased multicultural tolerance, both at the high school and college levels, much in same way that studies suggest that improving students' civic, cultural, and racial literacies leads to an increase in their overall level of tolerance.[6]

One of the most comprehensive policy documents analyzing religion in the social studies curriculum in the pre-9/11 era, published jointly by the Council on Islamic Education and the First Amendment Center, advocates chiefly for the anthropological notion of promoting religious tolerance as a chief reason for the study of religions.[7] The work of Diane Moore similarly lays out a case for the secular study of religion in the American context and, in particular, sees the multicultural tolerance afforded by studying religions to be especially valuable in combating Islamophobia.[8] Moore details various ways in which religion might be integrated into social studies, including the phenomenological approach, the literary approach, the historical approach, the cultural studies approach, and an approach based on multicultural education. In Moore's view, not all approaches are equally palatable in the public school setting. For example, though the phenomenological approach provides "a sympathetic introduction to religious traditions that is accessible to the novice," it is overly sympathetic to the reality of religious phenomena. Further, it has the major flaw of "reinforcing the common and deeply problematic assumption that religions somehow exist outside of their social/historical contexts."[9] Here, she is directly pushing back against Rudolph Otto and Mircea Eliade and their phenomenology of religion.[10]

Perhaps Moore's greatest contribution to the existing literature, besides placing herself very clearly in the anthropological camp, is her recognition that religion, like other cultural categories, has inherent normativity. She notes that "as a white person who has grown up in a society that values whiteness, it is difficult for [her] to recognize the ways that social norms, customs, and values privilege whiteness in our culture as normative."[11] For Moore, teaching about religion as a part of developing multicultural tolerance is about dismantling privilege, much in the same vein as Peggy McIntosh's classic work "The Invisible Knapsack."[12] Just as McIntosh attempted to make others aware of racial privilege, Moore hopes to raise awareness of the privilege that is inherent in religion, specifically the Protestant and Catholic faiths of Western Europe and the United States. Consequently, one must spend time both building—but more importantly, deconstructing—the category of "religion," particularly as it relates to categories of normativity and ethical judgements imposed upon it by Christians in the West.

The particular notion of combating the specific form of religious intolerance known as Islamophobia is explored in further detail in Moore's chapter entitled "A Case Study: Teaching About Islam."[13] Islamophobia is also explored in the writing of Charles Haynes and Oliver Thomas, who note that

> almost weekly now, United States citizens read in newspapers or see on television reports of "Muslim terrorist" threats or attacks aimed at some "enemy of Islam." The news-media drumbeat has led many of us to the false impression that the Muslim faith is a religion built on a foundation of violence and fanaticism. Nowhere have most of us been taught about the history of Islam or what Muslims today actually believe.[14]

Haynes and Thomas go on to suggest that their words were important even in the pre-9/11 world, but are particularly relevant today. More recent research explores the ethical obligations of teachers in public and Christian schools to actively push back against these harmful cultural and religious stereotypes.[15]

Although it is the most accepted significant rationale for the study of religions, there is some dissent around the idea that teaching religions can bring about multicultural tolerance.[16] It has been suggested that, in fact, when not given proper training, teachers who were allowed to simply teach about religion often over-promoted Christianity, generalized about other religions, and harmed the ability of students to develop tolerant attitudes.[17] Many other studies have found that teachers lack proper training in teaching about religion, lending credence to the argument that the wrong kind of teaching will actually leave the students worse off than no teaching at all, and perhaps intensify rather than ameliorate intolerance.[18]

Robert Jackson presents a detailed case for why the study of religion is important in the context of the secondary school curriculum, but holds a similar pessimism for using religion to increase multicultural tolerance.[19] He notes: "I do not think that any approach can solve the problem of deep seated racism. However, I do think that having an understanding of the religious culture of people in our societies might be a necessary, though not a sufficient, condition for reducing racial and cultural prejudice."[20] Jackson grounds his argument in the Orientalist framework of Edward Said and the cultural anthropology of Clifford Geertz, and argues that the impact of the study of religion on promoting tolerance and acceptance of diversity is diminished by essentialized definitions of religion and culture.[21] Here Jackson squarely aligns himself with the general Orientalist critique of Western education as well as the critiques of Moore, in that they are all critical of a process that emphasizes "the exotic, the other, the different, perpetuating the approaches of early social and cultural anthropologists."[22]

Although Jackson is concerned primarily with problematizing the study of religions as it currently stands, he does offer a few suggestions for how the curriculum might be improved. Drawing on Geertzian notions of culture, Jackson suggests that religion is "internally highly variegated" and as such, these distinct forms must not be so readily conflated with one another.[23] Practically speaking, this means that "ethnographic studies of religious communities," namely, focusing on the actual lived religious experience of contemporary practitioners, must be a more significant part of the public secondary school curriculum.[24] In doing so, the varieties of religious experiences might be more fully transmitted to students, in that they will come to understand the true diversity both in religious praxis and belief. This notion has been echoed by Keith Barton, who notes that the social studies field needs to "move beyond the 'major religions'" to "explore the diversity within religions" and the "changes in religion over time."[25] In addition, social studies education is so steeped in an anthropological approach to religion that religion is often seen as coterminous with culture.[26] Barton notes that "it is common to refer to Muslims as Arabs, Indians as Hindus, or Americans as Christians, but ethnic and political boundaries rarely coincide neatly with religious ones."[27]

In many ways, the need for specificity in understanding religious and cultural differences as outlined by Jackson and Barton can be seen in practice in the work of William Gaudelli, who recounts a moment whereby a Guyanese student of Indian descent who was religiously Muslim revealed her religious identity to classmates. When her classmates expressed surprise at this reveal, the student herself noted that "this just goes to show you that they don't have a good idea of what is happening in the world." She continued on, remarking how "they just assume everyone who is Muslim is either Arabic or black."[28]

Apart from grounding the study of religions in building global citizens or increasing tolerance, there is the argument that learning about other religions and other cultures is inherently beneficial for students. Moore grounds her desire to create a vibrant learning community centered on the study of religion with the notion that "religious literacy entails the ability to discern and analyze the fundamental intersections of religion and social/political/cultural life through multiple lenses."[29] In essence, religion fills out and illuminates further what is meant by social studies— that is, studying culture both here in America and internationally. In addition, Moore suggests that the study of religion allows students to understand the worldviews of religious people and thus prevents the students from falling into the trap of believing that "religious worldviews" are inherently "unsophisticated and irrational."[30]

The critiques of Moore, Douglass, and Jackson of essentialized, ahistorical, and tokenized renderings of religions other than Christianity are clearly on point, especially when one looks at recent curricular policy documents. The 2013 Common Core aligned *C3 Framework for Social Studies State Standards* attempted to address problems of this ahistorical approach, fostering a curriculum based more on inquiry.[31] However, the standards overlooked and marginalized religious studies—until a 2017 addendum focused on religion specifically.[32]

## STUDYING RELIGION AS A *SUI GENERIS* PHENOMENON

While anthropological definitions of religion are popular, there are scholars and educators, rooted in phenomenology of religion, who contend that religion is a category unto itself. Rudolph Otto bases his definition of religion around the term "the numinous," a feeling of awe and terror towards something greater than the self, as something that is a pre-rational part of religion and not based on belief or rationality alone.[33] For Otto, the numinous can only be experienced and it is an irreducible feeling, one that cannot be expressed adequately in the written or spoken word, or any other form of human communication. In Otto's mind, it is so essential for a scholar of religion to be able to connect with the "numinous" that he writes in the opening pages of his tome that "whoever cannot do this, whoever knows no such moments in his experience, is requested to read no further."[34] For Otto, one cannot really, in a truly authentic way, understand the religious experience without having had that experience for themselves. He continues, noting that "it is not easy to discuss questions of religious psychology with one who can recollect the emotions of his adolescence, the discomforts of indigestion, or, say, social feelings, but cannot recall any intrinsically religious feelings."[35] Here, Otto is clear to make the distinction that religion is a unique category unto itself. Religious feelings are not the same as social feelings, nor for that matter are they the same as the discomforts of indigestion or the emotions of adolescence. That said, although Otto calls the religious feeling "non-rational," he makes an important distinction to not ascribe to religiosity "the tendency of our time towards an extravagant and fantastic 'irrationalism'."[36] Instead, he goes to great lengths to describe the constituent elements of the numinous, the so-called *mysterium tremendum et fascinans* (tremendous and fascinating mystery) that comes to be associated with the divine.[37]

Otto and his successor Eliade contend that religions make specific, unique claims about the nature of the world, and that the religious and secular minds operate in markedly different ways from one another. For them, it is not simply, as Durkheim would argue, that religions clothe their worldviews with "an aura of factuality,"[38] but rather that

> ...religious man's desire to live in the sacred is in fact equivalent to his desire to take up his abode in objective reality, not to let himself be paralyzed by the never-ceasing relativity of purely subjective experiences, to live in a real and effective world, and not in an illusion.[39]

This is in direct contradiction to Durkheim and Geertz, who primarily see religion as one subset of the phenomenon known as culture.

While there is a large body of educational literature that implicitly uses an anthropological definition of religion in line with Durkheim and Geertz, there is likewise a compelling case to be made for seeing religion as a unique phenomenon. A phenomenological definition of religion presents different reasons for why religion is an important part of social studies, and in addition, raises a new set of challenges. While Meira Levinson's work focuses more broadly on civic education, she devotes a few pages to the way that religion can and should enter the social studies classroom. In a vignette that mirrors the larger debate between anthropology and phenomenology of religion, she recalls a moment when a student-teacher was organizing a debate on same-sex marriage. "Throughout 2005 and 2006," she notes "legal tussles over this initiative were in the news frequently."[40] At its core, Levinson and her student-teacher were in opposition to one another in terms of what arguments could be used in the classroom. Levinson argued that all arguments, both religious and secular, were permissible, while the student-teacher, drawing on the ideas of John Rawls, asserted that public reason does not allow for the open expression of such opinions.[41]

In a comparable vein, in documenting the way in which Islam was discussed by students in the classroom and then surveying personal opinions about the religion privately, the work of Gaudelli reveals a similar divide. During class, Mary, a Coptic Christian from Egypt, "made no comments, evaluative or otherwise, about Islam."[42] Gaudelli does not speculate on the reason for Mary's silence, but it may well have been on grounds outlined by Levinson—namely that public reason does not allow for the open expression of such opinions. In the classroom, Gaudelli notes, "teachers approached religion gingerly, trying not to offend students of various denominations, abiding closely to the principle of cultural relativism." Despite the tolerance of the classroom, "students, however 'polite' in the public sphere of the classroom, often revealed their utter disdain for religious groups other than their own in the private setting of an interview."[43] This was the case for Mary, who privately expressed her intolerance of Islam. In creating a safe space to discuss religion, teachers had perhaps afforded too safe a space, where the real issues, the real points of religious conflict and discord, could not be engaged and, perhaps, reformed.

These illustrations from Levinson and Gaudelli suggest not only that religious individuals have different perspectives from their secular peers, but more importantly, that they sometimes accept different axiomatic facts about the supernatural and the natural world and permit different questions to be asked about these facts.[44] Cognitive research suggests that the divide between religious and secular individuals exists even from an early age.[45] Not only do students of religious faith believe in the realness of religious stories more than do their secular counterparts, they also have less of an ability to discern fact from fiction in stories that involve general supernatural plot devices like magic and spells. The work of Gottlieb and Wineburg continues this line of research with adults, charting the impact of religious identities on the historical thinking of experts in various fields. Most importantly, their work helps in understanding how those with religious convictions read history differently from their secular colleagues by employing a series of categories to describe how these experts navigate their positions as both scholars and members of a faith community.[46] For those with religious identities, the concept of membership was very important, as they would much more frequently qualify their reading with "'as a historian' or 'being a Christian,'" demonstrating that their religious perspectives altered the way they read and interpreted the historical narrative.[47]

If classroom teachers are to take the phenomenology of religion seriously, it means (in line with Levinson and contra Rawls) that we must allow viewpoints based on religious views precisely because they are genuinely held and believed, whether we agree with them or not. Ultimately, religions shape how individuals—both youth and adults—see the world, and how they make sense of it. Of course, the main challenge in public schools is the wall between church and state, thus whether allowing religious viewpoints around civic questions is a bridge too far.

## CRITIQUING THE NOTION OF "RELIGION"

Recent writings in which Keith Barton have questioned inherent Christian normativity in which other religions are made to look more like Christianity and the differences between various sects of a religion are ignored. Barton argues that "religion" should be explored as a categorical phenomenon, so as to expose the ways in which "other" religions have been shoe-horned into the (consumerist) Christian mold.[48] Brent Nongbri disputes these same problematic, axiomatic assumptions in the field of religious studies in suggesting that "religion" is a construct of Christianity and the West.[49] Yet, besides his work, real critiques have not yet permeated the mainstream of secondary social studies education. The presumption of religion as a sui generis concept is particularly problematic for phenomenologists of religion like Otto and Eliade. After all, although Otto and Eliade are writing for the purposes of showing the universality of religion as manifest in a variety of religious traditions, they begin with categories and notions that are particularly understandable to post-Enlightenment Protestant Christians.

The very idea of religion as a "phenomenon" strips religion of its link to its cultural, social, and historical roots. Particularly in Enlightenment and post-Enlightenment Christianity, belief is more important than praxis, in which orthodoxy, or proper beliefs, supplants orthopraxy, or proper conduct. By assuming religion to be a universal phenomenon, conceptual categories derived from Christianity, like the *axis mundi* and the divide between the sacred and profane, are more likely to be inscribed upon religions that bear only a passing resemblance to the Christian tradition. In discussing the *axis mundi*—that is, an object imbued with sacred power, a so-called "hierophany" around which the profane world revolves and organizes itself—one sees this process in action.[50]

For Eliade, religions form around foundational centers that provide constancy and order in a complex and volatile world. This foundation is formed through the repetition of ritual, in the cycles of days, weeks, and years, as well as through the social community that makes up a religion. Eliade posits that all religions have places and objects around which their respective world revolves. For Muslims, this is the Kaaba in Mecca toward which all the faithful pray five times daily; and for Jews, this is the Temple Mount in Jerusalem. Eliade's notion of the *axis mundi* is convincing because of the variety of examples he uses to "prove" its universality. He unpacks Indian and Greek myths, describes rituals of Polynesia, and quotes the writings of the early Christian Church and a host of other sources from various times, places, and cultures to bolster his case. Yet ultimately, Eliade's "universal" concept fits particularly well with Christianity, as the person of Jesus Christ and the cross represent the Christian axis mundi, the point at which the heaven joins the earth, and around which life and ritual is organized.[51] Paul Hedges notes that some critics take their critique of Eliade further. He asserts that "Eliade exaggerated the significance of marginal myths to make them seem like universal patterns of religion while also distorting elements of various stories to fit a common predetermined narrative that he believed all axis mundi images should exhibit."[52]

Hedges argues that Eliade breaks the "first methodological rule"—namely, to remain aware of the dangers of seeing, or making, patterns which do not exist."[53] Let us turn back to Barton, who contends that religions are made to look more like Christianity than they actually are. Barton's point here is germane, seeing how the cultural systems most distinct from Christianity—be it Nazism, Scientology, or American football—are most akin to being evaluated as to whether they are, in fact, a religion.[54] Religions most unlike Christianity are understudied by the field.[55] Even concepts like "Native American Religion," while embraced by the academy as a whole, is disputed by some Native scholars.[56] Tink Tinker, for example, contends that "Native society has the formality of a religion thrust upon it."[57] Furthermore, he argues:

> ...the invention of religion in the late 19th christian century enables a close (academic) inspection that participates in the larger colonial project of control and power over the colonized Other by parsing out bits of a People's culture into bytes that might be better understood by eurochristian onlookers.[58]

Tinker here is arguing with anthropologists of religion, asking provocatively, "Is tying my shoes part of a religion?[59] After all, he asks, "Where is the dividing line between religion and not-religion? Do not all acts suddenly become religious? If all of life and every personal as well as community act is religious, then what can religion possibly be in this context?"

Conversely, the question "Is Christianity a religion?" is one almost never asked in academic circles. Problematizing any cultural category such as nationality, ethnicity, race, or gender, is an important part of any pedagogical experience of teaching and learning in the social sciences.[60] Problematizing religion is an important piece of content that is often left out of the equation, not only in the post-secondary academy, but also in the secondary social studies classroom. This push for critical thinking and critical questioning is an essential and inexorable part of any truly robust social studies classroom.

## CONCLUSION

A significant amount of research still remains to be done concerning the role of religion in the secondary social studies classroom. Though two main strands of literature emphasizing anthropological and phenomenological approaches permeate the current body of literature, the extent to which these theoretical justifications have permeated actual classrooms remains to be seen.[61] In fact, very little of the existing literature in the field of social studies education around the study of religion explicitly references these two foundational religious studies paradigms. While the existing literature engages with them implicitly, very rarely are they overtly explored. Further, there is still the need to address the question of both how and why teachers integrate religion into the social studies curriculum. What are their justifications for the study of religion and what approaches are actually used? Do practicing teachers define religion to their students more as a cultural phenomenon or as something that is altogether different from culture? These are important questions for a number of reasons.

One of the major issues when studying religion is that even the most readily accepted definitions of religion fail to precisely pin down what religion *is* in a way that possesses real and unique meaning. In the anthropological definition of Geertz, one can find very little that distinguishes religion from culture. In fact, anthropologists of religion see religion as one among many other cultural systems that provide order to society through a series of symbols and rituals. How can students understand what religion means if some of its leading proponents can hardly distinguish it as something separate from culture?

Phenomenologists of religion, focusing more on the individual believer than on the larger cultural milieu, alternatively contend that religion is best defined on the basis of its unique and irreducible character. Religion is not simply analogous to national or ethnic culture, although there might be overlaps. Yet for the phenomenologists, there is a similar ontological vagueness.[62] Phenomenologists leave non-believers on the outside, as for them, true understanding and certain types of religious experiences are inexorably linked.

Ultimately, of course, teachers are left with very little guidance on which is the "right" approach, if such a thing exists altogether. However, simply understanding their existences and engaging in this important conversation is an important first step, and will no doubt lead to more fruitful conversations with and among students about the role that religions play in our history, society, and culture.

## FOR REFLECTION

1   What is the difference between an anthropological understanding of religions and a phenomenological one? Which understanding do you find more common in your experience and why do you think that might be?

2   How does the category *religion* fail to describe the lived experiences and histories of the traditions we call *religious*?

3   How do you teach about religions in your own classroom? Are there any new perspectives you now want to engage?

# NOTES

1. Avishag Reisman, "Reading Like a Historian: A Document-Based History Curriculum Intervention in Urban High Schools," *Cognition and Instruction* 30 no. 1 (2012): 86–112; Russell J. Dalton, *The Good Citizen: How a Younger Generation is Reshaping American Politics* (Washington, DC: CQ Press, 2009).

2. Lawrence Sullivan, *Religions of the World: An Introduction to Culture and Meaning* (Minneapolis: Fortress Press, 2012).

3. Emile Durkheim, *The Elementary Forms of Religious Life* (New York: Dover Publications, 1912), 47.

4. George Monbi, "America is a Religion," *The Guardian*, July 29, 2003.

5. Clifford Geertz, *The Interpretation of Cultures* (New York: Basic Books, 1973), 90.

6. Emile Lester & Patrick Roberts, "Learning about World Religions in Modesto, California: The Promise of Teaching Tolerance in Public Schools," *Politics and Religion* 4, no. 2 (2011): 264–88; James Banks, "Diversity, Group Identity, and Citizenship Education in a Global Age," *Educational Researcher* 37, no. 3 (2008): 129–39; Merry Merryfield & Binaya Subedi, "Decolonizing the Mind for World-Centered Global Education," in *The Social Studies Curriculum: Purposes, Problems, and Possibilities*, ed. E. Wayne Ross (Albany: SUNY Press, 2006), 283–94; W. Smith, "Not Stopping at First: Racial Literacy and the Teaching of Barack Obama," *Multicultural Perspectives* 16, no. 2 (2014): 65–71; A. Vetter and H. Hungerford-Kressor, "'We Gotta Change First': Racial Literacy in a High School English Classroom," *Journal of Language and Literacy Education* 10, no. 1 (2014): 82–99.

7. Susan Douglass, *Teaching About Religion in National and State Social Studies Standards* (Nashville, Tennessee: Council on Islamic Education and First Amendment Center, 2000).

8. Diane Moore, *Overcoming Religious Illiteracy: A Cultural Studies Approach to the Study of Religion in Secondary Education* (New York: Palgrave Macmillan, 2007).

9. Moore, *Overcoming Religious Illiteracy*, 63–88.

10. See Rudolph Otto, *The Idea of the Holy* (Oxford: Oxford University Press, 1917); see also Mircea Eliade, *The Sacred and the Profane: The Nature of Religion* (New York: Harcourt Brace Jovanovich, 1957).

11. Moore, *Overcoming Religious Illiteracy*, 77.

12. Peggy McIntosh, "White Privilege: Unpacking the Invisible Knapsack," *Independent School* 49, no. 2 (1990): 31–35.

13. Moore, *Overcoming Religious Illiteracy*, 139–63.

14. C. Haynes and O. Thomas, *Common Ground: A First Amendment Guide to Religion and Public Schools* (Nashville: First Amendment Center, 2007).

15. John Shekitka, "Teaching About Religions in the Social Studies Classroom: The Post-9/11 World and the Post-Truth Age as Superstructures," *Journal of Research on Christian Education* 31, no. 1 (2022).

16. Philip Barnes, "The Misrepresentation of Religion in Modern British (Religious) Education," *British Journal of Educational Studies* 54, no. 4 (2006): 395–411.

17. Derek Anderson, Holly Mathys, and Joe Lubig, "Lessons Learned from Teaching Teachers How to Teach About World Religions," *International Journal of Learning, Teaching, and Educational Research* 10, no. 3 (2015): 43–58.

18. Kevin Burke and Avner Segall, "Christianity and Its Legacy in Education," *Journal of Curriculum Studies* 43 no.5 (2011): 1–28; Jennifer Hauver James, *Religion in the Classroom: Dilemmas for Democratic Education* (New York: Routledge, 2015); Melissa J. Marks, Russell Binkley and James K. Daly, "Preservice Teachers and Religion: Serious Gaps in Religious Knowledge and the First Amendment," *The Social Studies* 105, no. 5 (2014): 245–56.

19. Robert Jackson, "Religious Education's Representation of 'Religions' and 'Cultures,'" *British Journal of Educational Studies* 43, no. 3 (1995): 272–89.

20. Jackson, "Religious Education's Representation of 'Religions' and 'Cultures,'" 272.

21. Edward Said, *Orientalism* (New York: Random House, 1978); Geertz, *The Interpretation of Cultures*.

22. Jackson, "Religious Education's Representation," 276.

23. Jackson, "Religious Education's Representation," 282.

24. Jackson, "Religious Education's Representation," 284.

25. Keith Barton, "Reconsidering Religion in the Curriculum," in *Religion in the Classroom: Dilemmas for Democratic Education*, ed. Jennifer Hauver James (New York: Routledge, 2015), 61–78, especially 64–68.

26. Mett Buchardt, "When 'Muslim-ness' is Pedagogised. 'Religion' and 'Culture' as Knowledge and Social Classification in the Classroom," *British Journal of Religious Education* 32, no. 3 (2010): 259–73.

27. Barton, "Reconsidering Religion in the Curriculum," 65.

28. William Gaudelli, *World Class: Teaching and Learning in Global Times* (New York: Routledge, 2003), 117.

29. Moore, *Overcoming Religious Illiteracy*, 56.

30. Moore, *Overcoming Religious Illiteracy*, 34.

31. National Council for the Social Studies, *The College, Career, and Civic Life (C3) Framework for Social Studies State Standards: Guidance for Enhancing the Rigor of K-12 Civics, Economics, Geography, and History* (Silver Springs, MD: NCSS, 2013).

32. National Council for the Social Studies, "Supplement on the Academic Study of Religion Added to C3 Framework," socialstudies.org.

33. Otto, *The Idea of the Holy*.

34. Otto, *The Idea of the Holy*, 8.

35. Otto, *The Idea of the Holy*, 8.

36. Otto, *The Idea of the Holy*, 21.

37. Otto, *The Idea of the Holy*, 12–40.

38. Durkheim, *The Elementary Forms of Religious Life*.

39. Eliade, *The Sacred and the Profane: The Nature of Religion*, 28.

40. Meira Levinson, *No Citizen Left Behind* (Cambridge, Massachusetts: Harvard University Press: 2012), 201–02.

41. John Rawls, *Political Liberalism* (New York: Columbia University Press, 1993).

42. Gaudelli, *World Class: Teaching and Learning in Global Times*, 115.

43. Gaudelli, *World Class: Teaching and Learning in Global Times*, 75.

44. Brent Abrahamson, and Fred Smith, *Teaching About Religion in History Classes: Sacred and Secular History* (Brookfield, Illinois: Teachers' Press, 2000).

45. Kathleen Corriveaua, Eva Chen, and Paul Harris, "Judgements about Fact and Fiction by Children from Religious and Nonreligious Backgrounds," *Cognitive Science: A Multidisciplinary Journal* 39 (2015): 353–82.

46. Eli Gottlieb and Sam Wineburg, "Between 'Veritas' and 'Communitas': Epistemic Switching in the Reading of Academic and Sacred History," *Journal of the Learning Sciences* 21, no. 1 (2012): 84–129.

47, Gottlieb and Wineburg, "Between 'Veritas' and 'Communitas," 92.

48. Barton, "Reconsidering Religion in the Curriculum."

49. Brent Nongbri, *Before Religion: A History of a Modern Concept* (New Haven: Yale University Press, 2013).

50. Eliade, *The Sacred and the Profane, The Nature of Religion*, 12.

51. Eliade, *The Sacred and the Profane, The Nature of Religion*, 61, 136–38.

52. Paul Hedges, *Understanding Religion* (Oakland: University of California Press, 2021), 266.

53. Hedges, 266.

54. Stanley Stowers, "The Concepts of 'Religion', 'Political Religion' and the Study of Nazism," *Journal of Contemporary History* 42, no. 1 (2007): 9–24; Stephen Kent, "Scientology and the European Human Rights Debate: A Reply to Leisa Goodman, J. Gordon Melton, and the European Rehabilitation Project Force Study," *Marburg Journal of Religion* 8, no. 1 (2003): 1–35; Jonathan Haidt, *The Righteous Mind: Why Good People are Divided by Politics and Religion* (New York: Random House, 2012), 287.

55. Simon Taylor, "Symbol and Ritual under National Socialism," *The British Journal of Sociology* 32, no. 4 (1981): 504–20.

56. Joel W. Martin, *The Land Looks After Us: A History of Native America Religion* (Oxford: Oxford University Press, 2001).

57. Tink Tinker, "Religious Studies—The Final Colonization of American Indians, Part 1," *Religious Theory: E-Supplement to the Journal for Cultural and Religious Theory,* http://jcrt.org

58. Tink Tinker, "Religious Studies—The Final Colonization of American Indians, Part 2," *Religious Theory: E-Supplement to the Journal for Cultural and Religious Theory,* https://jcrt.org/

59. Tink Tinker, "Religious Studies—The Final Colonization of American Indians, Part 2."

60. Mett Buchardt, "When 'Muslim-ness' is Pedagogised." See also, Emily A. Daniels, "Racial Silences: Exploring and Incorporating Critical Frameworks in the Social Studies," *The Social Studies*, 102 (2011): 211–20; Joy L. Johnson & Robin Repta, "Sex and Gender: Beyond the Binaries," in *Designing and Conducting Gender, Sex, and Health Research*, eds. John L. Oliffe and Lorraine Greaves (Thousand Oaks, California: SAGE Publications, 2012), 17–37.

61. Durkheim, *The Elementary Forms of Religious Life*; Geertz, *The Interpretation of Cultures*; Otto, *The Idea of the Holy*; Eliade, *The Sacred and the Profane: The Nature of Religion.*

62. See Otto, *The Idea of the Holy*, 8.

# Part II

# <u>Practice</u>

# 6
# DEVOTIONAL PRACTICES IN PLURALISTIC SPACES
## Learning about Religions in Independent Secondary Schools

*Brian T. Blackmore*

In pursuit of leveraging religious literacy towards the civic-minded goals of shaping a more informed, harmonious, and pluralistic society, educators and researchers have identified public schools as the context in which they might have the greatest impact on making cultural and social change. One axiom of teaching about religions in public school contexts is that a teacher's approach must be nonsectarian and nondevotional. It is often said that religious literacy educators in public schools do not "teach religions" but rather they "teach *about* religions." The distinction between teaching religions and teaching about religions was defined by the Supreme Court when it outlawed mandatory spiritual or religious practices in schools in *Abington vs. Schempp* (1963) and the distinction has been further clarified by leading experts in the field of religious studies education.[1] The nondevotional approach for which the Supreme Court and leading experts have advocated is important for the successful operation of public schools because it is the only way that teachers can be assured they are teaching in ways that are constitutionally responsible and ethically sound.[2]

Given my experience as a teacher in an independent school founded on the principles of Quakerism, I would argue that the omission of religious and spiritual practices as the gold standard for all forms of religious literacy education should be reconsidered. Teachers in independent schools have opportunities for experiential learning that are simply constitutionally impermissible in public school contexts. It is worth examining what is pedagogically valuable about the visceral and affective ways that students in independent schools can learn about religions through an embodied and experiential encounter with spiritual and religious practices. Research demonstrates that high school students who have some experience with yoga, meditation, and mindfulness practices are more focused in their classes, develop skills for managing stress and anxiety, and improve their attendance and academic performance.[3] It is a matter of hotly contested public debate as to whether school instruction in these historically spiritual disciplines can be purely nondevotional. Regardless, independent school teachers are not bound by the same constitutional parameters as public school teachers and thus have greater latitude in terms of the kinds of religious practices they can incorporate into their lessons and learning activities. Based on my survey of research by experts in the field of religious studies education in secondary schools, a decade of experience teaching about religions in an independent school context, and conversations I have had with hundreds of independent school educators through the Center for Spiritual and Ethical Education and the Institute for Teaching about World Religions, I propose that spiritual and religious practices should not be so staunchly avoided in the design and implementation of curriculum for learning about religions in an independent school context.

What follows is a defense of the inclusion of spiritual and religious practices in the independent school *curriculum*—especially practices that support the well-being and psycho-social-emotional development of young people or have been proven to be pedagogically effective at advancing the goals of religious literacy education. I recommend several approaches that are sensitive and responsive to the wide diversity of orientations toward religion among the students we teach. I describe this pedagogy as "devotionally pluralistic" because it endeavors to embrace what is most civically important about religious literacy education with an appreciation for experiential learning and religious diversity.

The first approach is a simple centering exercise. Every class I teach begins with the low hum of a singing bowl followed by a short period of silence. The silence intends to offer students respite from the busyness, anxiety, and stress that is a constitutive part of the experiences of all secondary school students in contemporary America. Without words, I invite students to still their minds, slow down their bodies, and reflect on what they are experiencing in the moment. I often observe them expressing appreciation for this moment by audibly and visibly exhaling. Some students use this time to connect with a divine presence—however known. Meanwhile, others take advantage of an evidence-based opportunity to improve their psychological, emotional, and physical health.[4] A few students are unsure about what to do with this time, but they know to sit quietly with respect and patience. The silence ends with a brief expression of my gratitude: "Thank you, friends."

Students from a diverse array of religious and nonreligious backgrounds demonstrate comfort and appreciation for this practice because its cultural and religious dimensions are, depending on one's interpretation, ambiguous or even nonexistent. It is difficult to say whether the exercise of ringing a bell and settling into silence is uniquely Quaker, Buddhist, a combination of both, or something else altogether. Which traditions can rightfully lay claim to this practice, if any at all? Conclusive answers are not available to us and through that complexity and ambiguity is an opportunity for teachers to offer students a practice of welcome, inclusion, and belonging that meets them where they are. Practices like these intend for students to have a spiritual experience, but they are simple enough and structured in a way that students do not fear that they are participating in cultural appropriation or the commodification of a religious tradition. Nor do nonreligious students feel as though a religious or spiritual worldview is being imposed, because which religious or spiritual worldview would that be? Indeed, this exercise is accessible to a great diversity of students, because nearly anyone can find value in entering into silence, slowing down, and reflecting on what is happening in the present moment. Students in my classes come from a wide array of religious and non-religious backgrounds and I have not observed any conflict with this exercise vis-à-vis the tenets and responsibilities of their religious traditions.

Students at Westtown School (West Chester, PA), where I taught formerly, have varying and growing degrees of religious literacy. Hence, their perceptions regarding the origins of the bell-and-silence excercise are wide-ranging—and may change. First-year students take an Introduction to Quakerism course. While doing so, they might initially associate the bell and silence only with the Quaker tradition. Therefore, it is imperative that teachers in our department explain that using a bell is not the traditional way that Quakers initiate quiet during what is called Meeting for Worship, but it is nonetheless a common practice among some Quaker religious studies educators in their classes. Later in our program, students learn that this practice is not unique to Quakerism. All upper-level students at Westtown are required to take a full semester course on religious traditions that stand in the minority in the United States, namely Hinduism, Buddhism, and Islam. Therefore, upper-level students may begin to notice resemblances between the practice of ringing a bell followed by silence at their Quaker school with similar practices they are learning about in some Hindu and Buddhist traditions. This assumes, of course, that they do not already have deep familiarity with these kinds of Hindu and Buddhist practices from their own personal experience and backgrounds, in which case those connections would be made by them much earlier. The bell and silence is but one example of how students can experientially find connections between the development of their religious literacy and an embodied practice.

A second example of my teaching about religions through practices relates to Buddhism's Noble Eightfold Path—specifically, the Buddha's teachings on Right Speech.[5] I challenge my students to spend a full week speaking only when what they are about to say is truthful, necessary, and kind. If what they are about to say does not meet these noble criteria as defined by the Buddha, they should refrain from speaking. At the end of each day, they complete a homework assignment in which they journal about their successes and failures attempting Right Speech. As the week progresses, students question what it means to be truthful, necessary, or kind. Is a candid response, when one truly dislikes another person's outfit, an act of kindness? Are jokes necessary? Is omission of information the same as dishonesty? These are just some of the questions my students ask during their week of Right Speech. Their confessions of frustration provide a learning opportunity, a chance for me to invite students into a dialectical relationship with Buddhist Dharma. I ask them to define the criterion of truthful, necessary, and kind speech for themselves and to continue practicing.

The practice of Right Speech seems to have universal accessibility. The three values of truth-telling, simplicity over excess, and kindness are not exclusive to Buddhist religious traditions. And yet, the practice of performing Right Speech and the instructions that the Buddha gave about Right Speech have religious origins. Critical reflection about why Right Speech might feel more appropriate in a classroom setting relative to other practices can be deepened through an examination of the discipline from which teaching about religions in secondary schools emerged.

In *The Invention of World Religions*, religious studies scholar Tomoko Masuzawa argues that concurrent with the great schism in the Dutch universities that separated *Religionswissenschaft* (science of religion) from theological studies, the term "world religions" emerged during a debate among European academics concerning the classification of the so-called "lesser" and "higher religions."[6] Cornelis Petrus Tiele (1830–1902), a professor at Leiden University, proposed that ethnically and geographically specific faiths should be called "lesser" or "national religions," and religions that feature believers from across ethnic and national boundaries should be called "universalistic" or "world religions." Tiele and his contemporaries understood Buddhism as a religion with teachings that could be incorporated into any cultural context; meanwhile, Judaism was a religion that was specific to the Jewish people. Similarly, Christianity was thought to be universal, but Islam specific to Arab cultures and people.

This new classification system, and the term "world religions" that stems from it, have generated many problems. What evidence is there to prove a religion is inherently universalistic? Could a religion become universalistic over time? Is a religion's universalism a matter of socio-historical fact or theological principle? These are murky waters that independent school teachers should wade through if they wish to use devotional practices with a historically religious origin in their classrooms. Evidently, the kinds of religious practices typically included in a religious studies course at an independent school, and those that are not typically included, track along a similar mapping of the world, and the "world religions," as devised by the *Religionswissenschaft* in the late nineteenth century.

With some reservation and this fraught history of the "world religions" paradigm in mind, I still advocate for Right Speech exercises as well as yoga, meditation, and mindfulness in independent school classes. Many Americans believe that yoga, meditation, and mindfulness are nonreligious, but not everyone by any measure is comfortable with that claim. Religious studies scholars, practitioners of Hinduism and Buddhism, and critics of yoga, meditation, and mindfulness have all asserted these practices have religious origins, and in some cases enduring religious dimensions when practiced in secular contexts. Cathy Gunther Brown has studied the many legal debates involving the instruction of yoga and meditation in public schools and argues for them to be recognized as religious in nature. She notes that, in 1988, an important case in Arkansas determined that "yoga is a method of practicing Hinduism;" another case from 1995 classified the "Hindu-Yoga spiritual tradition" as a "religious tradition." Earlier cases, such as *Malnak v. Yogi,* determined that an elective high school course on Transcendental Meditation could not be taught because it was unconstitutional according to the establishment clause of the First Amendment.[7] The question of whether the practice of yoga in schools is "religious" continues to spark public debate and controversy. In 2013, a San Diego Superior Court Judge ruled against concerned (mostly Christian) parents who sued the school district claiming mandatory yoga classes in elementary schools were a form of religious indoctrination. The judge concluded that yoga is a religious practice, but not in the way it was taught by the San Diego school district. Yoga and meditation may also be the most widespread religious practices found in schools in the United States. Bethany Butzer, a psychologist with New York University, found that over 5,400 teachers were teaching yoga lessons in over 940 schools in 2015 and those numbers seem to be rising.[8]

The question for independent school teachers is not whether yoga, meditation, and mindfulness are *permitted*, but rather whether teaching about yoga, meditation, and mindfulness are universally accessible practices. And if so, does their incorporation into the religious studies curriculum suggest a difference in value between these practices and others which students might perceive as more culturally or ethnically specific? In other words, an educator's adoption of yoga, meditation, and mindfulness in their curriculum, without a similar approach to practices from other religions (for example, Muslim salat, Catholic sacraments, or Hindu puja), might give students the impression that some religions are more universal—and, by association, more enlightened simply by virtue of their universality—than others.

Some religious practices do not belong in a school setting. Many religious practices should not be performed by people who do not identify with the tradition from which that practice comes. In my work leading professional development programs for independent school educators of religion, I strongly discourage teachers from any attempt to imitate, or misappropriate in any other way, rituals and practices of traditions that are not their own. Most educators I work with are sensitive to the needs of their students and aware of the problems with cultural appropriation and religious commodification in their classrooms. Nonetheless, they (and myself included) must further examine the cultural hierarchies that are being reinforced when some religious practices (or practices that seem secular but have their roots in religious origins) are practiced in the classroom because they are deemed universal, but others are not.

A third approach to teaching about religions through practices was suggested to me by Katherine Zubko, Associate Professor of Religious Studies at University of North Carolina, Asheville, during a workshop for independent school teachers of religion hosted by the Center for Spiritual and Ethical Education in conjunction with the American Academy of Religion. At this event, Zubko invited her audience of teachers to consider how they might include more embodied learning and kinesthetic exercises into their religious studies courses. She also shared an excerpt from her article in *Sensing the Gods: Utilizing Embodied Pedagogy to Understand Hindu Devotion* in which she describes how she uses "the bodied movement grammars underlying practices at the center of particular religious traditions" as a tool for teaching about the affective and emotional dimensions of Hindu myths. While most approaches to teaching about Hindu myths start with a text or series of texts, and sometimes a look at visual representations of Hindu deities portrayed in sacred narratives, Zubko takes a different approach. She starts by introducing her students to the "bodied movement grammar" of the nine *rasa*s, a principle of South Asian aesthetics which relates to human emotions and moods. She assigns each group one of the *rasa*s and asks them to imagine situations in which they might experience the feeling of emotion or mood associated with that *rasa*. Students role-play the situations they surmised and record observations of facial expressions and gestures displayed by one another during live-action role-plays.[9]

It is only after preliminary experimentation with *rasa*s that Zubko introduces students to a Hindu text. She observed that student experience with embodying the *rasa*s first helped them later develop sophisticated insights into a particular story about an old woman ascetic who offers Lord Rama a fruit as an offering after tasting it. Her documentation of the richness and depth of her student's critical reflection is worth quoting at length:

> Students who only read the story often are puzzled as to why it would matter that Shabari samples the fruit first, and if it was such a violation, why Rama would accept the half-eaten fruit. By experiencing the mechanisms of disgust within the embodied aesthetic framework of rasa, students make more sophisticated observations about Shabari as a devotee who intentionally takes on the possibility of encountering sour or bitter in order to locate the sweetest offering, purposefully dismissing societal conventions (a typical rhetoric at the heart of bhakti), and creating an intimacy of shared food often reserved for close family members or lovers. Rama also becomes a god who invites affection in compassionate, in sometimes unorthodox ways, and is not bound in his choices by rigid purity systems. Being able to recognize these aspects of affection, as grounded in their own bodied knowledge, opens up a multidimensional understanding of bhakti.[10]

For Zubko, who teaches at a public institution, it is essential her students know that "we are not practicing religion, [but rather] we are using practice to learn about religion." Zubko's approach to teaching about religions through "movement grammars" may also be helpful for independent school educators who are interested in using more experiential learning in their curriculum, but concerned about cultural appropriation.[11]

For example, rather than asking students to perform Muslim prayer in Arabic five times a day, teachers could ask students to set an alarm on their phones to ring at five designated times during a 24-hour cycle and when their alarm rings they could recite a short poem of their choosing. This approach gives students an opportunity to experience one of the "grammars" of Muslim prayer without being asked to perform it. Taking another example: instead of asking students to participate in a Jewish Seder, students could be asked to design the menu for a special meal commemorating a historical event in which social injustice was overcome by a community to which they feel connected. How should the food on the table be set and how should the chairs be arranged? What foods should be presented on the table but not eaten? What foods should be consumed? What sequence should they be consumed in, what should be said, and what gestures or actions should the dinner guests expect to make during the meal? These questions help students think critically about the affective, emotional, and theological dimensions of the Seder meal for Jewish people. If students host the meal that they have designed, they might uncover more insights about Jewish religious experience through "the bodied movement grammars" of Pesach without the teacher ever asking (or requiring) students to perform a religious ceremony.

In her essay on embodied pedagogies for teaching about Hindu myths, Zubko highlights the work of Michelle Mary Lelwica, professor of religion at Concordia College, who incorporates Aikido, a Japanese martial art, into some of her religious studies courses. Lelwica writes: "Bringing the body into the process of learning about religion introduces a kind of epistemic diversity that changes—and potentially enriches—our understanding of religious practices and beliefs by revealing the creative role the body plays in the construction of religious meaning." A class on religions bereft of kinesthetic and experiential learning, notes Zubko, through the work of Jennifer Oldstone-Moore, simply misses "the power and transformative nature of the multisensory context of religious practice."[12]

Teachers in independent schools and educators working in other contexts outside of the public school system have an opportunity to improve religious literacy in ways that go beyond knowledge acquisition about religions and the development of abilities to interpret the role of religion in the world. Teachers of religion in independent schools are uniquely positioned to give students an opportunity not just to think about but to feel the affective, embodied, and emotional dimensions of religious experience. Doing this work in a diverse multireligious educational setting can be complicated and fraught with mistakes, but I believe strongly that cultural appropriation and religious commodification can be avoided if independent school teachers exclusively incorporate practices like the ones described above. These are practices that (a) are not culturally or religiously tied to a particular religious tradition, or (b) are widely assumed to be universally accessible, or (c) feature the bodied movement grammars of religions without asking students to practice specific religious rites or rituals. If the primary aim of civic-minded religious literacy education is to create a more informed and ethically responsible citizenry, then religious practices—when adopted with expert care, thoughtfulness, and critical reflection—can be skillfully incorporated into the religious studies curriculum in order to support the fulfillment and fruition of a more harmoniously pluralistic world.

## FOR REFLECTION

1   What do students gain from approaches to religious-literacy education that incorporate embodied practice(s)?

2  How noteworthy is the difference between religious practices that are deemed acceptable in an educational context and those that are deemed unacceptable? Why does this distinction exist? In what ways does the distinction influence how certain religions are taught?

3  Where is the line between experiential learning and imitation or appropriation of religions and cultures?

# NOTES

1. In 1988, with the support of a broad coalition of seventeen religious and educational organizations, the distinction between an academic nondevotional approach to the study of religion and a devotional approach to religious studies was further clarified by the First Amendment Center and the prohibition against religious practices in the curriculum was reinforced. The First Amendment guidelines for teaching about religions in schools have stressed that, in part, "the school's approach to religion is academic, not devotional," and, "the school sponsors study about religion, not the practice of religion." See Charles C. Haynes and Oliver S. Thomas, *Finding Common Ground: A First Amendment Guide to Religion and Public Schools* (Nashville, TN: First Amendment Center, 2007). In April of 2010, the American Academy of Religion (AAR) adopted these guidelines as "a useful thumbnail sketch" in the publication of its own: *Guidelines for Teaching about Religion in K–12 Schools in the United States* (April 2010). More than ten years later, it remains one of the few authoritative standards for teaching about religion in K–12 public schools produced by religious studies scholars.

2. See Charles C. Haynes and Oliver S. Thomas, *Finding Common Ground*. See also, Diane L. Moore, *Overcoming Religious Illiteracy: A Cultural Studies Approach to the Study of Religion in Secondary Education* (New York: Palgrave Macmillan, 2007); *American Academy of Religion Guidelines and Religious Studies Companion Document for the C3 Framework* (Institute for Curriculum Services, 2017).

3. See C. C. C. Bauer, C. Caballero, E. Scherer, M. R. West, M. D. Mrazek, D. T. Phillips, S. Whitfield-Gabrieli, and J. D. E. Gabrieli, "Mindfulness training reduces stress and amygdala reactivity to fearful faces in middle-school children," in *Behavioral Neuroscience* 133, no. 6 (2019): 569–85; Satya Prakash Purohit and Balaram Pradhan, "Effect of yoga program on executive functions of adolescents dwelling in an orphan home: A randomized controlled study," in *Journal of Traditional and Complementary Medicine* 7, no. 1 (April 20, 2016): 99–105; R. J. Semple, et al, "A Randomized Trial of Mindfulness-Based Cognitive Therapy for Children: Promoting Mindful Attention to Enhance Social-Emotional Resiliency in Children," in *Journal of Child Family Studies* 19 (2010): 218–29;

and N. N. Singh, et al, "Effects of Samatha Meditation on Active Academic Engagement and Math Performance of Students with Attention Deficit/Hyperactivity Disorder," in *Mindfulness* 7 (2016): 218–29.

4. J. C. Felver, et al, "A Systematic Review of Mindfulness-Based Interventions for Youth in School Settings," in *Mindfulness* 7 (2016): 34–45.

5. I offer gratitude to Kevin Eppler, former teacher and Department Chair at Westtown School, for sharing this effective teaching technique with me.

6. Tomoko Masuzawa, *The Invention of World Religions, or, How European Universalism Was Preserved in the Language of Pluralism* (Chicago: University of Chicago Press, 2005), 1.

7. Cathy Gunther Brown. "The debate over yoga and mindfulness in schools," *PhillyVoice* (May 13, 2019).

8. Bethany Butzer, et al. "School-based Yoga Programs in the United States: A Survey," in *Advances in Mind-Body Medicine* 29, no. 4 (2015): 18–26.

9. Katherine C. Zubko, "Sensing the Gods: Utilizing Embodied Pedagogy to Understand Hindu Devotion," in *Religious Studies News: Spotlight on Teaching* (October 27, 2016).

10. Zubko, "Sensing the Gods."

11. Zubko, "Sensing the Gods."

12. Zubko, "Sensing the Gods."

# 7

# BRIDGE-BUILDING IN SECONDARY EDUCATION
## The Case of a Youth-Led Community Organization

*Taha Vahanvaty*

During the years following the 2016 presidential election, I became increasingly concerned about the rise of political, religious, and social division within the US and more specifically amongst teenagers. Our nation was embroiled in a civil war of ideas and identities. Social media has turned all conversations about race, religion, identity, and politics into battlefields, and the front lines were filled with pundits from all sides stoking the flames of polarization. This polarization made it impossible for a society to govern itself and prevented us from addressing our most pressing problems, such as a global pandemic and foreign conflict. A recent article by Carol D. Lee, Gregory White, and Dian Dong makes this point:

> As vital public institutions, schools have not been unaffected by these developments. Schools have seen an increase in political awareness and activity, and research has shown that rates of bullying, aggressive behavior, bigotry, and harassment have risen in recent years. Increasing polarization and division in society, as well as the ubiquitous availability of questionable digital information, have also made civic reasoning and discourse skills progressively more important for students to develop. These skills are essential to cultivating as students prepare for their future roles as adults, citizens, and being full members of their varied communities. Increasing polarization is also being further exacerbated by

growing inequality and the deleterious effects that this has on the learning and civic development opportunities for vulnerable and alienated students.[1]

Motivated by concerns about polarization similar to those highlighted above, I started an after-school club in 2017 at Stroudsburg Junior High School while I was in eighth grade. The club's name was The Acceptance Project (TAP) and its mission was to build empathy and understanding across differences. However, identifying how to tangibly and effectively achieve this goal required a steep learning curve, especially in a school environment like Stroudsburg Junior High School. The school is located in northeastern Pennsylvania in Monroe County and is home to a politically diverse population of nearly 170,000 residents.[2] In 2016, 48% of the county voted for Trump and 49% voted for Clinton. The state's other elections also reflected election wins by similar razor-thin margins. While students in Stroudsburg Junior High School did not vote in the 2016 presidential election, their parents did. Echoes of the political division began developing in my school, compounded by racial tensions, partly caused by an increasingly diverse student population. The junior high school is home to about 800 students, 53% of whom are students of color; however, fewer than 1% of its 52 teachers are people of color.

For the first year (March 2017–March 2018), TAP meetings consisted of projects that—while well-intentioned—lacked structure, strategy, and direction. Once a week for ninety minutes, about fifteen students would meet after school to work on projects that were designed to bring the school together. Two examples of such projects were the Unity Board and the "Changing the World is in Your Hands" Mural. The Unity Board involved SJHS students writing their name on a slip of paper and attaching it to a section of a bulletin board that contained the name of their country of origin. Eventually, enough names would fill up the board resulting in students' names and places of origin merging, symbolizing a sense of interconnectivity among the students. For "Changing the World is in Your Hands," TAP members painted a mural that illustrated a globe being held in two hands. SJHS students then wrote random kind notes about their peers and stuck them onto the mural.

The random acts of kindness and harmonious actions the projects initiated undoubtedly provided students with brief moments of respite from the social, racial, and political polarization that surrounded their everyday lives.[3] However, the major flaw in these projects was that they focused solely on highlighting the similarities among students while ignoring the underlying tensions and differences that exist between them. There was no opportunity for students to engage in civil discourse about their differences and the controversial issues facing their communities and country. This was mainly because I did not know how to organize or facilitate a proper dialogue session, nor did I understand how to use it properly as a tool for peacebuilding.

In the fall of 2018, I entered my sophomore year at Stroudsburg High School. Although Stroudsburg it's student population was larger than the local junior high school's, it still reflected similar socio-economic and demographic trends. In a population of around 1,200 students, 48% were students of color and over 30% were on a free or reduced-price lunch plan.[4] I knew that, in order to increase TAP's effectiveness, I needed to research how other like-minded bridge-building organizations facilitated dialogue.

By the end of my sophomore year (June 2019), I had developed a model using strategies and formats for facilitating dialogue across differences from several organizations, universities, and experts. As a result, TAP meetings began to follow a more standard format wherein students with opposing viewpoints engaged in facilitated dialogue sessions about divisive issues such as religious freedoms, identity politics, gender, policing, and so on. The dialogue format was designed in the following way:

1. TAP members participate in a brief (often humorous) icebreaker. Icebreakers work very well for warming up the room, even for students who are already familiar with each other. An icebreaker can get people talking, generate laughter, and help participants start with an initial level of comfort.

2. The session then moves to "spectrum questions." We create a physical linear spectrum in the classroom allowing students to move to sections of the room titled Strongly Disagree, Disagree, Agree, Strongly Agree based on their response to what has been asked. It is challenging for young people to "think out loud" in a pressured situation, so this activity helps familiarize them with the practice of taking a position and defending it.

3. After all the Spectrum Questions have been asked, participants break out into random groups of five to seven. Once in these breakout groups, TAP officers repeat the Spectrum Questions, which the groups discuss—taking two or three minutes for each.

4, Once the breakout groups have concluded their discussion of the Spectrum Questions, everyone shifts their chairs into one large circle. This is where the bulk of the dialogue happens for the remainder of the meeting. Chapters usually allot one hour for this large dialogue circle.

Originally, TAP's mission statement was "To promote understanding, empathy, appreciation, and acceptance of different faiths, cultures, beliefs, and races. Our project allows us to learn from each other the core value of humanity that unites us all." However, I realized that this mission statement focused on finding solutions rather than reaching an understanding. An understanding is a mutual appreciation for one another's needs, fears, experiences, and hopes. Reaching an understanding is far more feasible than finding an immediate solution, but may nonetheless lay a foundation for future solutions and new relationships. As a result, by the end of my sophomore year, I changed TAP's mission statement to "Creating a new generation of empathetic leaders, active listeners, and creative thinkers by facilitating civil discourse in high schools."

The overall goal of TAP dialogues is to assist in the *development* of students' levels of empathy, confidence, active listening, critical thinking, and verbal communication. We accomplish this by giving students the space and the opportunity to practice the skill of airing a variety of different views while behaving respectfully towards one another. A successful dialogue need not result in opinions being changed. However, it will cause some students to consider fresh perspectives and realize that seemingly black-and-white issues may be more complex than they had previously thought. The process of civil discourse is more important than the product (reaching the "right" conclusion). If students express and listen to a variety of views on a controversial topic, and they do so civilly, then the discourse is a big success, regardless of any intellectual conclusion reached.

## The Acceptance Project Into Summer (TAPIS)

After creating a methodical dialogue model and renewing TAP's mission statement, I became eager to spread TAP chapters to other school districts in Pennsylvania. In the fall of my junior year at Stroudsburg High School (September 2019), I began developing "TAP Into Summer" (TAPIS): a one-week, all expenses paid, overnight dialogue intensive summer camp hosted at the Kirkridge Retreat Center in Bangor, Pennsylvania.[5] Through the program, students would be equipped with the necessary leadership and facilitation skills needed to start and run a TAP chapter back at their own high schools.

In October 2019, a local non-profit named Monroe County United (MCU) became TAP's fiscal sponsor, allowing me to apply for and receive a $15,000 grant from the Weiler Family Foundation. The bulk of the funds was used to cover TAPIS attendees' room and board. Summer camps that facilitate dialogue do exist across the country, but they often charge thousands of dollars to attend, making civil discourse a privilege for those with the means to engage in it.

Unfortunately, due to the Covid-19 pandemic and nationwide school shutdowns, my efforts to market TAPIS to students in surrounding school districts were stalled; I decided to postpone TAPIS to the summer of 2021. Meanwhile, I moved forward with a virtual training program. I picked six students from Stroudsburg and Pleasant Valley High Schools to participate in the TAPIS online. The training was six hours over a span of three consecutive days during July 2020. Both teams of students began running TAP chapters as TAP officers at their respective high schools in September 2020. Because I had developed this online training format, I was able to train students from other school districts who were not able to attend the TAPIS in person. Since 2020, I have trained five more students from Princeton High School (located in Princeton, New Jersey) and King's Academy (located in Amman, Jordan) through this virtual method. While the virtual training method enables me to reach far more students, I have found that it is not nearly as effective as an in-person training. A vital part of the in-person training is having students interact with one another and engage in challenging dialogue. The subtle details in students' body language and tone are lost through a Zoom meeting and can greatly hinder a facilitator's ability to navigate a difficult dialogue effectively.

Once life and school began to resume semi-normally in the fall of 2020, I decided to revamp TAPIS marketing. TAPIS had received media coverage and our promotional video reached over 17,000 people on Facebook.[6] However, it was my systematic referral-based marketing method that got students from other schools to apply to the program.

During my outreach efforts, I connected virtually with renowned international peacebuilder Dr. Paula Green.[7] In 2018, she founded an organization named Hands Across The Hills.[8] Through it, residents of Leverett, Massachusetts, and Letcher County, Kentucky, spent three weekends in each other's towns in an attempt to better understand each other. Recognizing our shared vision, I partnered with Hands Across The Hills and recruited two high school students from Amherst, Massachusetts, and one student from Letcher County, Kentucky, to attend TAPIS. Dr. Green also lent me her decades of peacebuilding wisdom and experience in developing the TAPIS facilitator and leadership training curriculum.

After months of planning, years of fundraising, and countless hours of marketing, fifteen students from across nine different school districts converged at the Kirkridge Retreat Center on July 28, 2021. For four nights and five days, these students participated in an agenda that consisted of team-building activities, guest speakers, and facilitator training sessions. All fifteen students successfully completed the training program. TAP now was active in five school districts and was being set up in five more.

## The Acceptance Project Focus Groups (TAPFG)

During the summer of 2020, the same time I was preparing for TAPIS, my school district, Stroudsburg Area School District, became a statewide epicenter for a slew of viral videos containing students saying racist and anti-black slurs.[9] Local issues relating to race and racial equity were further magnified by nationwide and local movements protesting the murder of George Floyd.[10] This community-wide racial reckoning was even further amplified by a Pennsylvania State Supreme Court Ruling named *Mahoney Area School District v. B.L.*[11] The court essentially ruled that students could not be disciplined by their school district for speech said off the school's campus, even speech that contained explicitly racist slurs and content. The result: a racially tense school district whose administration, faculty, and staff were unable to engage freely in dialogue about the very factors contributing to the school, community, and nationwide racial tension.

There was another factor contributing to the absence of any dialogue on race within the Stroudsburg Area School District classrooms. On one hand, socially liberal-leaning students, especially students of color, were uncomfortable sharing their thoughts on issues relating to race with their majority white teachers.[12] On the other hand, socially conservative-leaning students, especially white students, refrained from sharing their thoughts on issues relating to race for fear that they would mistakenly say the "wrong thing" and be highlighted on social media.[13] However, I knew that outside the classroom, students were still talking about issues relating to race. The problem was that they were solely communicating through their (mainly online) social bubbles.[14]

To initiate the conversation on race and racial equity in the school district and the community, I hosted a webinar on June 20, 2020, consisting of six local leaders from Monroe County Pennsylvania titled "Monroe County TAPs Into Race."[15] The panelists included State Senator Mario Scavello, Representative Maureen Madden, Monroe County Sheriff Ken Morris, MCU President Tom Jones, East Stroudsburg University Chief of Police William Parrish, and Stroudsburg Area School District Superintendent Dr. Cosmos Curry. The dialogue within the webinar centered on the more than 150 questions submitted to me anonymously by students about the following topics: Police Accountability, Privilege, Criminal Justice Reform, Free speech, and "Our Community and Us." While the webinar was no substitute for the in-person, peer-to-peer dialogue my community and school needed, it was a way to involve students indirectly in initiating the conversation on race.

The nationwide racial reckoning also forced school districts like mine to reexamine (and in many cases, begin to develop) their Diversity, Equity, and Inclusion policies. However, I knew that my school's policies needed more student-centered and student-generated data. I also knew that students in my school desperately needed to engage in conversations with each other about issues relating to race and racial equity. As a result, I created TAP's third program: TAP Focus Groups (TAPFG). TAPFG had two goals: to increase students' levels of empathy, confidence, active listening, critical thinking, and verbal communication; and to gather qualitative data on how Stroudsburg High School students felt and thought about issues relating to race and racial equity, so that we could better inform our school and district's diversity, equity, and inclusion policies.

I piloted the first focus group, "TAP Into Race" (TAPIR), at SHS.[16] Ten students were selected through an application process to participate in five consecutive, ninety-minute, weekly, after-school, dialogue sessions. The application selection committee consisted of two social workers from Pennsylvania Intermediate Unit 20, two teachers, the school's TAP volunteer community advisor, and the Stroudsburg Area School District director of curriculum.[17] I then hired a student facilitator from East Stroudsburg University's Diversity Dialogue Project to assist me in facilitating the focus group.

During each of the dialogue sessions, the TAP teacher advisor and two IU 20 social workers took extensive notes on students' verbal and nonverbal responses. I also created a TAPIR input form that participants filled out during the first, third, and last dialogue session to measure their levels of empathy, confidence, active listening, critical thinking, and verbal communication. Although all of this data was generated and gathered, it was not analyzed by a qualitative data expert nor was it formally presented to school district administrators or school board members. While the TAPIR pilot was successful, no focus groups have been organized by TAP at Stroudsburg High School or in any other school district TAP is based in. In fact, TAPFG program has been suspended indefinitely, due to liability and logistical challenges, as I explain further below.

## TAP MERGER WITH BridgeUSA

In February 2020 I connected with Manu Meel, the CEO of BridgeUSA.[18] This international, student-led organization was created in 2016 by Meel and his peers at the University of California, Berkeley, following the 2017 Berkeley riots.[19] Since then, BridgeUSA has been leading the fight against polarization and apathy amongst students across the country through college and high school chapters. By merging resources and communities from BridgeUSA and TAP, we have created a pipeline from the beginning of high school to the end of graduate school in which students practice civil discourse and engage across lines of difference. This merger offered current TAP chapters a newly expanded network of high school and college-age bridge-builders. Furthermore, TAP chapters now have access to a full-time working team, as well as informational and monetary resources to bolster each of their impact.

BridgeUSA has worked closely with me to connect TAP's existing ten chapters and members to create a network of students who are passionate about bridging our political divides through empathy and productive conversation. These chapters have been added to BridgeUSA's High School community, and their leaders are working with BridgeUSA to strengthen and grow their bridge-building efforts.[20] I am confident that this merger will have an incredible impact on youth bridge-building in our country that will be felt for years to come.

## Looking Ahead

TAP is not the first bridge-building organization to exist in this country, nor will it be the last. However, I hope that my experiences, reflections, and analysis can serve as a useful case study and sounding board for all future bridge-builders out there. Bridge-building is essential to the health of our nation and is needed now more than ever.

I could not be more hopeful for the future of bridge-building. At the grassroots are organizations like TAP and BridgeUSA that are combining resources, manpower, and ideas. On the legislative side, congressional bills are being passed to fight polarization head-on.[21] Education leaders across several states are working in tandem with lawmakers to create "depolarization" curricula.[22] National education organizations are publishing a growing body of research on civics and civil discourse specifically focused on public schools.[23] I am now a student at American University. However, I remain a part of BridgeUSA's network and a dedicated advisor to all existing TAP chapters. My years at TAP have fostered a deep-rooted passion for bridge-building that will likely propel me into a career path centering around conflict resolution and peace.

## For Reflection

1   Is peer facilitation worth the risk that it poses? Why or why not?

2   What is the role of dialogue in bridge-building? What are the elements of an effective dialogue?

3 In what ways does a young person's socio-economic background influence the degree to which they could benefit from after-school dialogue programs like TAP?

+ + + + + + + + + + + + + + + + + + + + + + + + +

# APPENDIX A: TAP METHODOLOGY

## ORGANIZATIONAL STRUCTURE:

*TAP Into Summer*: The objective of TAPIS is to train students on how to facilitate dialogue and how to start and lead a TAP chapter. The goal is to have students become TAP officers and start TAP chapters in their respective high schools.

*TAP Chapters:* The objective of TAP chapters is to have TAP officers organize and facilitate weekly discussions in their high school on a variety of pressing topics. The overall goal is to increase students' levels of empathy, confidence, active listening, critical thinking, and verbal communication.

*TAP Focus Groups*: After running their chapter for more than six months, the objective was for TAP officers to organize and facilitate a focus group in their respective high schools while working with a local college/university student with a background in facilitation. The goal was to gather qualitative data on how students are thinking/feeling about any pressing topic (race, gender, identity, and so on). By sharing this data with school administrators, TAP would be able to help schools develop student-centric Diversity, Equity, and Inclusion policies.[24]

## TAP CHAPTER MEETING STRUCTURE:

While each TAP chapter is run slightly differently, there is a fairly standard meeting and dialogue format they each follow. Before the dialogue:

1. TAP officer(s) will come up with a list of two or three dialogue topics that are in current events.

2. Members of the TAP chapter will vote on which topic they'd like to engage in a dialogue about.

3. TAP officer(s) will then draft a dialogue outline about the topic voted upon.

## TAP FACILITATOR TRAINING

Whether it was through a virtual training session or in-person at TAPIS, all TAP officers learned about leadership strategies, the basics of civil discourse, the logistics of how to start and run a TAP chapter at their high school, and how to facilitate group dialogue. However, the main focus of TAP's facilitator training is *educating students on how to ask well-positioned and well-crafted follow-up questions*. Thought-provoking questions produce more insightful information and deeper connections. Good follow-up questions show TAP participants that TAP officers are listening and that they are genuinely curious. Nothing builds trust faster than heartfelt interest in what another person is saying.

All TAP officers must complete three main "question-asking" workshops. The first is "The Art of the Follow-Up." It is important for student facilitators to move beyond *what* a student's opinion is and towards *why* the student has that opinion. In the information age, young people have a tendency to transform every dialogue into an exchange of statistics and "out-Googling" each other. This is because it is far easier to focus on facts than it is on feelings. While being informed about a topic is incredibly important, it is vital that students understand how their backgrounds, experiences, and emotions influence their beliefs, opinions, and viewpoints. TAP officers are trained to ask four types of follow-up questions to help them dig deeper and understand the "why" behind students' opinions:

1. **Ask for elaboration**: You want students to provide further details on their initial idea. Never hesitate to get someone to elaborate. In all the dialogues I've had, no one has ever said to me, "You already asked me that." So long as you ask respectfully and with genuine curiosity, people are happy to tell you more.

2. **Ask differently**: You want students to approach their idea from a different perspective. One way to follow up is to restate the initial question. There are a few techniques to generate these questions, such as using a synonym for a loaded word or putting the topic in the context of a specific event or incident so that the student can elicit more concrete insights and relatable stories.

3. **Ask about a related topic**: You think there is a connection to be made. By listening to someone's stories, you will realize how their life experiences influence their opinions, thoughts, and beliefs. When I ask about someone's story and I learn that their religion is the driving force behind their political opinions, I get the chance to learn about their faith system or cultural upbringing as well.

4. **Ask them to challenge assumptions**: You want to surface what is unsaid. When people make generalizations, they are usually saying more about their feelings or impressions of the thing than about the thing itself. Generalized statements like "That candidate's supporters are racist and ignorant" give you a chance to dig into these impressions.

In order to practice this lesson, students play a game called "Hot Seat." This activity teaches students how to think of follow-up questions quickly, how and when to ask open-ended questions, and how to ask questions that follow the flow of the dialogue.

The second mandatory "question-asking workshop" is called "Balancing Your Dialogues." In this activity, TAP officers learn how they can create balance by asking "liberal-leaning" and "conservative-learning" questions. Public speaking is difficult for most high-schoolers. This difficulty is compounded by the fact that most teens find it daunting to voice unpopular opinions in public, especially in today's social and academic climate. It is unfair to expect one or two students to defend a particular position if thirty classmates are taking the opposing view. (A few bold, extroverted students may enjoy these odds, but most students will not.)[25] Because TAP's meetings are "open door," facilitators have no control over the type or number of students attending each dialogue. As a result, facilitators must know how to provide extra support to the students voicing a minority opinion. By asking liberal- or conservative-leaning questions, facilitators can make space during the dialogue for the minority voice so that they do not feel hopelessly outnumbered, cornered, or threatened.

- **Liberal-leaning question example**: "What can be done to ensure access to abortion in rural areas?" Assuming a liberal hypothetical for the question (abortion is already legal) makes it easier for a liberal-leaning student to answer.

- **Conservative-leaning question example**: "Why should the government involve itself in abortion?" Assuming a conservative hypothetical for the question (government *should* involve itself in abortion) makes it easier for a conservative-leaning student to answer.

In order to practice this lesson, students participate in an activity called "Balancing Act." Students are given a question about a socially or politically controversial topic, such as "Should abortion be legal in

America?" They are then given thirty minutes to come up with *at least* ten liberal-learning and ten conservative-leaning questions they would ask in a dialogue they would be facilitating about that question.

The third required workshop, used only during TAPIS, is called "We're Not Really Strangers" (WRNRS). This is "a purpose-driven card game and movement all about empowering meaningful connections. Three carefully crafted levels of questions and wildcards that allow you to deepen your existing relationships and create new ones."[26] Players draw cards containing thought-provoking questions, such as "When was the last time you lied to your mother?" and "What is a dream you have given up on?" It was the perfect game to help teach students how to dig deeper into someone's story.

Every day during TAPIS, I would randomly split students into five groups of three. I would give them an hour to play WRNRS. On the first day, each group received ten cards. All the groups got through the ten question cards within the first twenty to twenty-five minutes. However, they had been instructed they had to stay sitting in their groups until the hour was complete. Some groups sat awkwardly in silence for about 30 minutes on the first day, and others gingerly tried to make small talk to fill up the time. On the second day, all the groups finished their ten question cards, but took about forty-five to fifty minutes. On the third day, the majority of the groups easily filled up the hour and got through only five question cards. On the fourth and fifth days, no group discussed more than three cards. This showed me that students would ask each other the questions on the cards, then follow up with their own inquiries. By the end of the week, students were confident, comfortable, and curious enough to continue personal and difficult conversations with one another without the help of the WRNRS question prompts.

## Appendix B: TAP Marketing

The secret behind getting a diverse group of students to attend either TAP chapter meetings, TAPIS, or the TAPIR Focus Group is referral-based marketing.[27] The issue of gathering a diverse group of individuals for a dialogue plagues every bridge-building organization. On a national scale, the majority of individuals that participate in bridge-building initiatives are liberal-leaning, above 60, retired, upper-middle-class, and white. However, I've realized that the best chance of getting a conservative-leaning individual to attend a dialogue session is if their friend is attending and if that friend is encouraged to draw in that individual for a meeting. Hence, the referral-based marketing strategy.

In order to draw high school students to a TAP meeting, TAP officers are trained to have a targeted system of reaching out to specific students. Before each meeting, they will review a pre-made list of students they believe are conservative-leaning, liberal-leaning, and students whom they think don't hold any strong positions on the dialogue topic. By creating a list of student names, TAP officers are able to hold themselves accountable for who comes. This tactic has proven to be the most effective at getting students to attend TAP chapter meetings.

I used a similar tactic on a larger scale when recruiting students across North Eastern Pennsylvania to apply for TAPIS. I advertised TAPIS by having a team of two or three students "cold email" teachers at high schools across that region and "cold direct message" high school students. [This method of personal outreach was the reason every student who attended TAPIS applied in the first place.]

For the TAP Into Race (TAPIR) focus group, I was able to gather such a diverse group of participants for the focus group because I deliberately and personally encouraged students from different social circles to apply. Although I was not a part of the participant selection process, it was because of my outreach efforts that a diverse racial, social, and ideological group of students applied and eventually participated in the focus group dialogue sessions.

## Appendix C: TAP Strengths and Weaknesses

An analysis of *The Acceptance Project* reveals that some of its strengths and challenges are not specific to it, but rather are characteristics of the entire youth bridge-building movement in the country.

### Facilitation Training

TAP focuses the bulk of its facilitation training on *teaching student facilitators on how to ask well-positioned and well-crafted follow-up questions*. This is a strength, because it enables me to effectively equip students with a very specific set of skills. While question asking is not the sole technique needed to run a constructive dialogue session, it is critical because it cultivates traits that are necessary for an effective facilitator—such as curiosity, active listening, balancing conversations, and keeping conversations flowing. If you are able to ask good questions, these skill sets will come naturally.

Yet, training high school students to become facilitators presents a unique set of challenges. Unlike college students, they have far more rigid schedules and are constantly balancing other life responsibilities. These factors prevent them from making TAP a primary priority. As a result, it is difficult to expect total reliability from TAP officers.

In addition to logistical concerns, student facilitators can sometimes be ill-equipped to facilitate certain dialogues, even after going through the training. At the end of the day, the best training comes from facilitating real life dialogue sessions. However, an inexperienced facilitator can potentially cause damage to TAP's reputation, to their TAP chapter's reputation, and to the emotional health of the students participating. In fact, facilitation requires real-life practice, but it also poses the risk of serious damage. It is of paramount importance to maintain quality control over facilitators, because they are the linchpin of TAP's peace building efforts. However, that is far easier said than done.

### Use of Extracurricular Chapter Model

Bridge-building in America is currently operating piecewise: over 400 bridge-building organizations in the country are doing similar, if not the same, work.[28] While grassroots efforts are necessary and valuable to reduce polarization and increase understanding across differences, they cannot be the only peace-building methods this country relies upon. I believe all bridge-building organizations that currently exist should make an effort to consolidate their efforts. While I have had countless individuals aid me in developing and growing TAP, I had been running the day-to-day operations largely by myself. By making arrangements to merge with BridgeUSA, I made sure that TAP operations continue to run under a far more sustainable infrastructure. Having a full-time paid team manage all current TAP chapters and officers ensures that TAP's mission can continue to live on without me.

Merging with a larger grassroots organization like BridgeUSA is the first step toward making youth peacebuilding sustainable and scalable. However, grassroots dialogue efforts are not enough. Any community or extracurricular organization will only be able to draw in a limited number of participants. Furthermore, students who participate in extracurricular activities typically tend to be from wealthier backgrounds. This means that bridge-building's largely volunteer-based model of participation is inherently inequitable. In order for bridge-building to be truly effective and equitable, policymakers and leaders in education need to develop a national curriculum that educates youth on civic reasoning and discourse. Leaders within the "system" and grassroots organizations need to work *together* in order to lay a foundation of peace within our youth. This strategy of peacebuilding is elaborated on by John Paul Lederach, developer of a peace-building pyramid demonstrating that relationships are one key against violence. The pyramid consists of three levels in peacebuilding: 1) the grassroots level, where people work for peace from the bottom-up; 2) the leadership level, where people work top-down for peace; 3) the middle level, in which people from both the grassroots and leadership work for peace. From explaining to his students how the middle group of people works, Lederach gradually developed the peacebuilding pyramid into a networking web approach to peacebuilding.[29]

## TAP Into Summer

Through TAPIS, students grew immensely in some of the following categories: public speaking; communicating thoughts and feelings about complex issues; how to be authentic and honest about one's experience; overall confidence in oneself; active listening; asking questions to dig deeper into someone's story; and storytelling. We were successful in creating an environment that gave students enough confidence and courage to be vulnerable, push themselves far outside their comfort zone, and openly wrestle with nuanced issues such as police accountability, gender norms, religious values, and so on. Furthermore, because room and board were covered by TAPIS, over half of our participants were from a low-income background and came from Title 1 schools, enabling us to achieve our goal of making civil discourse more accessible. Here are some examples of testimonials given by TAPIS participants:

- "This camp taught me 1) How to facilitate discussions in a way that is balanced and includes everyone; 2) How to ask follow-up questions to get to the deeper information than what someone might offer up, to begin with; 3) How to remain level-headed, and try to understand where people are coming from instead of making snap judgments."

- "It was so incredible to get to meet all these new people who come from different backgrounds and have different opinions from me, but still be able to connect to everyone on such a deep level and make some amazing friends. I also feel like I learned so much about how to be empathetic and understanding, as well as practical leadership skills."

- "I made so many new friendships and got to have meaningful conversations that people my age don't normally get to have."

- "TAP was a positive outlet for me to express my feelings on harder topics, and it helped me realize that people (especially my age) are capable of having a non-aggressive discussion. Plus, I got to meet amazing people at TAP that will forever have a positive impact on my life."

While TAPIS was quite successful, it did have challenges. Marketing TAPIS and getting students to apply was difficult. It involved experimenting with different marketing avenues such as reaching out to school teachers, principals, faculty, leaders of religious youth groups, Boy Scout troops, and other extracurricular organizations; cold messaging students on social media; sharing information on Facebook groups; and reaching out directly within my larger social circle. As stated above, word of mouth was most effective. However, it was especially difficult getting conservative-leaning students to apply, resulting in a group that was not as ideologically balanced as I would have liked—with twelve out of fifteen participants self-identifying as liberal-leaning.

## TAP Into Focus Groups

The pilot TAPIR focus group was a success because it brought together from my school a group of students who were diverse in terms of race, gender, and ideology; these students would have otherwise never sat down with one another and talked about race. An example illustrating how diverse the participants were is that we had students who had gone viral on social media for saying racial slurs sit across from the students who "exposed" the videos on social media in the first place. Despite the tense, difficult, and (at some points) uncomfortable dialogue, all the participants answered that they would participate in a focus group again.

I initiated TAP Focus Groups with the vision of creating a student-led model of generating, gathering, and analyzing focus group data in order to further inform school districts' DEI policies. TAP officers would generate the data (facilitating conversations), social workers would gather the data (note-taking), and qualitative data experts would analyze the data. However, the steps that I took to secure official approval for this focus group were laborious at best. Having minors facilitate focus groups composed of minors brings up unique liability concerns, and the data generation and analysis process require professional expertise that is often difficult to acquire, especially on a pro bono basis. Unless TAP officers were paid and had further training specific to running a focus group, it is unreasonable to expect them to carry out research through this model.

# NOTES

1. Carol D. Lee, Gregory White, and Dian Dong, "Educating for Civic Reasoning and Discourse," *National Academy of Education*, (2021): 3–4.

2. "Monroe County, PA population by year, race, & more" in *USAFacts*, https//usafacts.org.

3. Rasmus Skytte, "Dimensions of Elite Partisan Polarization: Disentangling the Effects of Incivility and Issue Polarization," *British Journal of Political Science* 51, no. 4 (2021): 1457–75.

4. These statistics came from the 2018 version of "Overview of Stroudsburg High School – Pennsylvania," in *US News & World Report*.

5. Kirkridge was the perfect place to host TAPIS logistically and symbolically. For more than 75 years, this retreat center has provided a safe harbor for interfaith organizations to gather, pray, recoup, and organize. See kirkridge.org.

6. See Lisa Mazerealla, "Tapping into opposing viewpoints with respect and civility" (January 31, 2021), wvia.org.

7. See "About Paula," paulagreen.net.

8. See handsacrossthehills.org. See also, Paula Green, "Hands Across the Hills: Appalachians and New Englanders Build Bridges of Understanding and Care," in Lucinda Allen Mosher et al., eds, *Deep Understanding for Divisive Times: Essays Marking a Decade of the Journal of Interreligious Studies* (Newton Centre, MA: Interreligious Studies Press, 2020), 160–64.

9. Joe McDonald, "Student-led march set Saturday in response to racist video posted by Stroudsburg student," PoconoRecord.com (June 5, 2020).

10. Maria Francis and Ashley Catherine Fontones, "Stroudsburg honors George Floyd, Black Lives Matter movement," PoconoRecord.com, April 5, 2021.

11. "Mahanoy Area School District v. B.L. | Oyez," April 28 2021, https://www.oyez.org/cases/2020/20-255.

12. Laura Meckler and Kate Rabinowitz, "America's schools are more diverse than ever. But the teachers are still mostly white," *The Washington Post,* December 27, 2019.

13. Taylor Lorenz and Katherine Rosman, "High School Students and Alumni Are Using Social Media to Expose Racism," *The New York Times*, June 16, 2020.

14. Carrie James and Megan Cotnam-Kappel, "Doubtful dialogue: how youth navigate the draw (and drawbacks) of online political dialogue," *Learning, Media and Technology*, (2020): 45:2, 129–50.

15. Ashley Fontones, "Pennsylvania High School Students to Lead Webinar on Race," govtech.com, June 24, 2020.

16. If TAP had been able to run more focus groups they would have followed the same branding as TAP Into Race (TAPIR): TAP Into Gender, Immigration, Politics, and so on.

17. Intermediate units (IUs) serve students and schools by providing essential educational services, such as special education, online learning programs and support, preschool programs, professional development for educators, administrative and purchasing consortia and much more. See https://paiu.org.

18. BridgeUSA, "About Us," www.bridgeusa.org.

19. Katy Steinmetz, "Fighting Words: A Battle in Berkeley Over Free Speech," *Time* (June 1, 2017).

20. BridgeUSA, "Press Release April 25, 2022", www.bridgeusa.org, April 25, 2022, https://www.bridgeusa.org/press-release-april-25-2022/

21. Derek Kilmer, "The Building Civic Bridges Act," kilmer.house.gov (February 9, 2022).

22. Adam Hoffman, "Civic Discourse," tea.texas.gov.

23. Carol D. Lee, et al., "Educating for Civic Reasoning and Discourse," 3–4.

24. As stated earlier, the TAP Focus Groups (TAPFG) program has been indefinitely halted due to liability and logistical challenges.

25. While there is no specific de-escalation training, students are trained in decreasing the "temperature" of the room: Knowing how to recognize a student's comment, actions, or body language to discern when they are agitated; being comfortable letting the agitated student having the space to "voice" their agitation; asking the dialogue group for silence to make breathing room for student's thoughts.

26. Available at www.werenotreallystrangers.com.

27. Referral marketing differs from pure word of mouth marketing in that it provides for tracking of referrals.

28. This claim is made by Listen First Coalition; see www.listenfirstproject.org.

29. See John Paul Lederach, *Building Peace: Sustainable Reconciliation in Divided Societies* (US Institutes of Peace, 1998).

# 8
# EMBRACING THEOLOGICAL MESS
## Two Rules for Teaching Religion

*Chase de Saint-Félix*

A few years ago, at a meeting of our Catholic high school's Gender and Sexuality Alliance Club, a young gay student named Roland steered the conversation in an unexpected direction.* Roland needed to unload a bit: he confessed that he was having a hard time in his Theology class on Roman Catholic Sacraments—not academically, but emotionally. As the class discussed foundational Christian practices like baptism, holy orders, and marriage, Roland felt increasingly ostracized from the material. Though he calls himself a (Protestant) Christian, Roland was beginning to think that the God he loved did not love him back in the same way. "I just have so many questions," Roland said. "I love Jesus, but I am not baptized, and the Church doesn't want me to get married." He told us that he probed his Theology teacher with almost daily questions on these topics. Will I go to hell if I'm not baptized? Can I still go to church if I marry another man? The teacher, he said, responded by pointing him to the catechism of the Catholic Church. Roland was less than consoled.

This wasn't the first time that Roland had a difficult time in Theology class. The previous year, his teacher was fond of holding classroom debates on controversial topics. Although the teacher saw himself as a detached, unbiased observer in these debates, Roland felt that they became forums for students to air their prejudices confidently, seemingly supported by the teacher and the material. When the class debated gay marriage, LGBTQ students stayed fearfully silent, while others felt

---

* Author's note: Names have been changed to preserve the anonymity of students.

empowered to describe their discomfort with queer people. When the class debated women in the clergy, most of the girls in the room were silent, while the boys by and large told the room that they found it hard to trust women in positions of authority. Obviously, these debates had not served to help students learn, but instead to make students feel unwanted.

I spoke with each of these teachers after I learned about these incidents. What had been the intent of these lessons? Were the learning outcomes achieved? Did they know the effects these lessons and these pedagogies were having on their already marginalized students? For the most part, each teacher had much the same response. This was a Catholic school, these were Theology classrooms, and the Catholic Church's position on these issues is clear. Neither teacher felt empowered or inclined to disagree with or challenge the Church's stance; each felt obliged to teach its theology *as is*. I wanted the teachers to consider the position of the students, but they wanted me to consider their position as catechetical instructors. These *are* the positions of the Church and these *are* the debates currently being held by the faithful. Who were they to teach otherwise?

At the time, I was hard pressed to remedy this impasse. But I found myself thinking about these topics again a few months later, at a meeting of our Institute for Islamic, Christian, and Jewish Studies teaching cohort. In our meeting, we were treated to a wonderful introductory lesson on Christianity. As a teacher of theology and religion, I never tire of these introductory lessons—although, by now, I've sat through more than I can count. When you've studied a religion for a long while, or even lived and practiced a religion for a spell, it can be hard to condense a complex and multifaceted faith into a brief and digestible introduction. I love watching people solve this little teaching puzzle.

This particular intro lesson was masterful. It focused on the long history of theological debate within the Christian tradition, complete with interweaving graphs and charts, and scattered with seemingly arcane phrases like *sola scriptura* and *filioque*. As a scholar of Christian history, I saw my own education reflected in this lesson. This was how Christianity was taught to me as a student. This is how most textbooks present Christianity to students. And this is how our school's content benchmarks ask us to teach Christianity to our students. In short, Christianity *is* its theology, and to understand the religion, you must understand how certain theologies became orthodoxies and how some became heresies.

But in this introductory lesson, I kept thinking about Roland. Specifically, I kept trying to find Roland in the twists and turns of this theological history. Sure, this was just an intro lesson; but what lesson would come after that? Would Roland find himself in that one? Or would it be the lesson after that? How far down the line would we have to go before he could see himself in this lesson plan? And if he did find himself, would it be an image of himself with which he would identify, or one too warped by exclusionary orthodoxies?

It's easy to think this is just about one student, or even one social identity. There are all kinds of Christian-identifying folk, however, who don't fit into this theological approach to teaching: devout students from single-parent households grappling with the Church's position on divorce; students from charismatic churches who rarely pick up the scriptures; young women told that they can never inhabit the person of Christ in the way a man can. If we insist on holding close to orthodoxy, if we insist on teaching only theology, then we leave out so many real, practicing religious people who don't completely fall into step with that theology. I'd be willing to bet that *most people* do not align easily with that orthodoxy. That doesn't make them any less sincere in their belief and devotion.

As the teaching profession continues to grapple with its own complicity in propagating harmful systems of oppression—especially in the wake of America's racial reckoning in the summer of 2020—it has become increasingly common to hear folks use the language of "mirrors and windows": students should be able to see their own lives reflected back to them in the curriculum; and they should gain insight into the lives of people different from themselves. While many humanities fields have made great progress in this area, Theology and Religious Studies still lag. As the stories I've related above make clear, the friction in these fields is coming from both student and teacher. On the one hand, teachers often feel compelled to present a monolithic, easily digestible orthodoxy to their students. Sometimes it's because a higher administrative power has asked us to do so. Sometimes it's because our textbooks present information that way as well. If we're honest though, mostly it is just that it's easier. It is so much easier to teach students about clean, clearly delineated theologies than it is to teach them about the messy, quotidian, lived experiences of real, faithful practitioners.

From the other side, students also ask teachers questions that entice a singular, up-or-down response. Think back to Roland's own queries: will I go to hell if I'm not baptized, or, can I still go to church if I marry another man? In their own desire to make sense of themselves and their place in religious communities, students ask us for something more concrete than "it depends on who you ask." As much as students may solicit these responses though, we as teachers need to see these questions as moments for reflection. Are we modeling religions in our classrooms in ways that elicit these types of questions? Would these types of questions begin to fade away if we showed religions and the faithful in all their true diversity and messiness?

As I've ruminated on these issues in my own teaching, I've begun to think more seriously about how I model religions for students and what my role in the classroom should be. As a product of these reflections, I've started my Religion classes this year with discussions of two rules for study, two guiding principles that I'd like students to keep in mind as they explore the lives of the faithful. Since these issues of representation in our Religion and Theology classes are generated by both student and teacher, inasmuch as these are then rules for students, they are also promises from me, standards to hold myself to throughout the semester.

The first, and less controversial of the two, flows naturally from the stories related thus far: if we begin a sentence with "This religion believes," we should assume that the end of that sentence is "except for all the practitioners who don't." When students know to expect diversity, when they are primed to see that the exceptions to a rule are often more common than the rule itself, it becomes far easier for them to make sense of things that might otherwise be tricky: the gay Catholic in the back row of Mass, refusing communion, fighting every day to exist in a Church that does not fully want him; the excommunicated women priests who continue to hold services; the young American Jewish person who aligns her sympathies with Palestine; the Muslim man who drinks alcohol and eats pork; or the Buddhist who treats a *bodhisattva* as a god. Not only does this approach have the benefit of presenting a more empathetic and holistic view of religion to students, it's also plainly more accurate than presenting straight orthodox theology. We cannot pretend that the lives of Muslims can be understood in any nuanced sense with just a straightforward discussion of the Five Pillars; that Judaism can be summed up by Torah and Talmud; or that Catholicism is merely the catechism. This first rule helps students see that there are religious people in both the fringes and the theological center of their faiths, and that in fact most religious people do not completely line up with "on paper" orthodoxy.

Depending on the type of school you work in, and on your own religious sentiments, the second rule may be harder to swallow. One final story will illustrate the need for it. I was once asked to attend a Safe Space training at American University, a training where teachers and students have conversations on how to make the school a more inclusive place for its queer populations. I was asked to attend because the topic of religion often comes up in this training and the facilitators wanted an opinion on how they might better engage with the topic. As the training swung toward religion, a young woman named Penny spoke up about her own experiences. As a lesbian from a more conservative town in the American South, she said that she'd often had occasion to debate her Christian neighbors on the topic of LGBTQ issues in the religion. "I like to point them toward the Old Testament," Penny said. "I tell them that there are all kinds of laws in the Old Testament that they aren't obeying, like rules against mixing fabrics or rules against eating shellfish. And I say that they are picking and choosing which rules to follow to suit their own prejudices. And that puts them in their place." Penny got a large applause after this, from a mostly queer and secular audience. I then chimed in with a question: "Does that ever work? Do you change minds with that approach?" Penny replied, "Not really; no."

The issue with Penny's approach is plain: she assumed she understood her neighbors' Christianity better than they did, that she could point out something they had not yet considered. To put it a different way, Penny was telling her neighbors that the standard of their faith should be their Bibles, specifically certain sections of their Bibles. But of course, that's not how all Christians ground their beliefs. It's not really Penny's place to tell her neighbors how they should think about their own religion. But while we might judge Penny for this frankly haughty approach, we should also turn that eye of judgment on ourselves as religion teachers. Do we not often do the very same thing in our classrooms, telling students the "correct" way to think about a religion? Do we not, just through our pedagogical practices, both implicitly and explicitly, present sets of standards for a religion that not all faithful people abide by? Is there even a way to avoid doing this?

Rule Number Two is my attempt at a remedy: no one is ever wrong about their religion and their faith. Although this rule is reminiscent of the subjective positions put forth by people like Kierkegaard, I think of it in more practical than philosophical terms. Internally, members of the same religion will of course have heated debates about the correct ways to live out their faiths. As teachers, we should also expose students to those debates and give them insight into the thinking of religious people. And yet, responsible stewardship of our students means removing the vocabulary of right and wrong, correct and incorrect, from our presentations of these topics. Instead, we have to use frames like mainstream belief vs fringe belief, laity vs clergy, populist vs hierarchical—if we are to get students to see how members of the same faith from different identities, regions, and demographics make up a complete mosaic of the religion.

I'll confess a bit of personal anxiety when I first started implementing these rules. Presenting religions in this fashion is, as I've said, a much messier enterprise. It certainly is not how religions were taught to me in school, not how textbooks present religions, and not how standards and benchmarks ask us to think about our teaching. But a single class activity helped me see the promises of this approach. I have often asked students to interview members of faiths we are studying in class, and to write up reflections on these interviews as homework. While, in the past, I might have had general class conversations on how those went, never before had I asked students to publicly share with each other the details of the particular opinions their interview subjects held. If I'm being honest with myself, a part of me was just nervous: what if someone they interviewed said that the stuff they were learning in class was wrong? This year, however, not only were students to present detailed accounts of the subject's views to the whole room, they were specifically directed to ask their subjects a key question: do they agree with the ways in which I as the teacher have presented the religion to the students?

With these changes to the activity, and with students already primed to think about our "two rules" for studying religion, the nature of the interviews changed fundamentally. While most interview subjects found my approaches to discussing their religions unobjectionable, some did! However, instead of students thinking that I had tricked them, or thinking that I didn't know what I was talking about, they started to have far more complicated and nuanced conversations with each other. Why did Jordan's interview subject care so much about scripture when Beckett's didn't? Why did Aniyah's subject think that Judaism was fundamentally about human relationships, while Anu's subject thought Judaism was all about the chosen people's relationship to the land of Israel? In the end, students became more curious about diversity in religions, more insightful in their evaluations, and more careful in their deductions. They became less prone to judge and more likely to empathize. To my great joy, the students also became more likely to see pieces of themselves in these religions, where previously they might not have. Selfishly, it also made my job way easier. Since implementing these rules, I have leaned into the mess, and much of the weight of needing to "get it right" is gone. It's not my job to present a false monolith, but to give students tools to navigate the richness of people's lived experiences.

## FOR REFLECTION

1   What about the two rules for teaching and learning religion do you find more difficult? Most promising?

2   What impediments might you encounter in your context to the "interview and report" assignment and how might you get around them?

3   What alternative to this "interview and report" assignment might work well in your context?

# 9

## CHRISTIAN PRIVILEGE IN PUBLIC SCHOOLS
### Non-Christian Teachers' Experiences

*Vicki A. Scullion*

Coach Kennedy walked out onto the fifty-yard line after the public high school football game, dropped to his knees, bowed his head, arranged his hands in traditional Christian prayer pose, and communed with his Christian God. During this time, students and teachers from both schools and other community members milled about on the field and in the stands, congratulating each other on their win or commiserating on their team's loss. Some sang the school's fight song and made plans to get pizza after the game. Many others joined the coach on the field to kneel in Christian prayer. The coach's prayer session after the game was a tradition, but the school board in Bremerton, WA worried that allowing it to continue might be a violation of the First Amendment's Establishment Clause. They asked him to stop the ritual. When he refused, the board suspended the coach from his teaching position. He sued, claiming that the school district had violated his right to freely exercise his religion.

Is there an obvious "correct" First Amendment answer to this disagreement? Not really. In the case known as Kennedy v. Bremerton School Dist. 21–418 (June 27, 2022), the U. S. Supreme Court found that the school district had violated Kennedy's right to free exercise of his [Christian] religion during his "free time" from teaching duties. In effect, by finding Kennedy's display of Christian prayer at a public school event legal, the Supreme Court sanctified the power of Christian privilege already present within public schools.[1]

Christian privilege is a result of the normative discourse that Christianity is the universal religion of the United States. In public education, for example, this discourse allows Christians to disregard as unimportant the diverse religious beliefs that teachers, employees, parents, and students bring into schools with them, and encourages them to openly privilege Christianity. Researcher Khyati Joshi has noted that Christian privilege "results in the oppression of members of religious minorities and atheists."[2] But, what does that oppression look like? I undertook a study, the intent of which was to add to the body of research literature on Christian privilege. By collecting and interpreting interview data from non-Christian teachers, I sought to understand how Christian privilege affects them while they are working in public schools.[3] My sixteen interview participants represent a broad array of non-Christian faiths and non-faith, among them teachers who self-identify as Muslim, Hindu, Jewish, Buddhist, agnostic, and atheist. Prospective participants who self-identified as culturally Christian were not included in this study.[4] At the time of the interviews, study participants lived and worked in three different county public school systems in north Georgia and taught in seven different schools, ranging from elementary to high school.[5]

All sixteen of my interviewees had stories to tell about various experiences with Christian privilege while working in public schools. Fifteen noticed Christian privilege in speech that Christian colleagues or administrators used while speaking to them. Fourteen received official school emails from colleagues that contained openly Christian content. Eleven mentioned that they had attended mandatory faculty meetings that opened with a Christian prayer. Six sat through mandatory presentations that included open Christian proselytizing. Nine dealt with restrictive policies or practices in the schools relating to the observance of non-Christian religious holidays. Ten reported being confronted by the Christian certainty of colleagues or students in ways that made it difficult to work with them.

Christian sentiments such as "I'll pray for you" and "Have a blessed day" were commonly expressed in public school spaces. Fifteen participants noticed that their colleagues and administrators felt comfortable and safe openly disclosing and promoting their Christian beliefs in the public schools. For example, Lauren (agnostic) and Emma (atheist) spoke about being exasperated by the common Christian sentiment, "I'll pray for you," because they saw it as a meaningless platitude. Lauren explained that "if I were to say, 'don't [pray for me]; do something else for me, like bring me dinner,' I think they would just be like *what*? And so I don't usually say anything." Bina (Jewish) and Ginny (atheist) both objected to Christian speech because they firmly believed in the separation of religion and state, and, therefore, found these statements inappropriate in a public school. However, Nathan (agnostic) appreciated the sentiment behind "I'll pray for you" comments. "I take it as a high compliment. They are relating my troubles to the highest entity that they could possibly think of so that he or she may help me. I think that is a very, very kind thought."

Nuha (Muslim), who wore a hijab with modest dress that covered all but her face and hands, was the only participant who did not observe Christian speech at school. She believed that it was because her colleagues strictly followed separation of religion and state guidelines, but it is possible that Christian colleagues may have been afraid of saying something to her that might be construed as negative or offensive. While her Christian colleagues outwardly respected Nuha's Muslim faith, they may have effectively segregated her from their personal group interactions by strictly limiting their overall communication with her to professional matters.

When Christian messages or prayers are communicated through public school channels, they do not pass unnoticed by non-Christian teachers. Fourteen participants mentioned that they regularly received official schoolwide emails advertising Christian prayer meetings and Fellowship of Christian Athletes prayer sessions or offering news about colleagues experiencing personal problems and requesting prayers. Not having to (re)consider religious content or a comment such as "I'll put the sick colleague on my Baptist church prayer list" before hitting "reply all" is a Christian privilege seemingly entrenched in official public school email communications in north Georgia.

Three of the participants in this study also noted that some of their Christian colleagues refused to remove Bible quotes from their email signature lines, even after they had been told in several school-wide faculty meetings and emails that First Amendment protocols at their schools prohibited them. The fact that this issue was addressed in school-wide meetings and emails, but was not necessarily enforced by the administrations when individual Christian teachers refused to comply, may suggest that administrators are unwilling to speak to these Christian teachers one-on-one about the issue. These participants especially worried about the marginalizing effects of the Bible quotes in emails sent to non-Christian students, parents, and stakeholders in the religiously diverse community.

Fumiko (Buddhist) was the only participant to bring the use of official school communication channels for personal religious purposes to the attention of the administration. She cautiously spoke to the person responsible for investigating discriminatory incidents at the school, who promised to keep her identity private. It was important to her that "[friends and colleagues] don't know that I've tried to call attention to what's going on through outside channels. I don't want the retaliation. I love my job." In her meeting with this administrator, she "expressed concern that school electronic communications were being used for someone's personal religious agenda, like for Fellowship of Christian Athletes stuff and teachers wanting to advertise for prayer meetings." While her objections to the use of school communication channels to promote individual Christian religious agendas were heard and some minor changes made, Fumiko ultimately felt that "my opinions don't really matter a whole lot in the big scheme of things, but at least I try to voice my opposition when I have a chance."

When asked the question, "Can you tell me a story about a time you felt that your religious identity might not fit into the dominant school culture?" eleven participants specifically referred to experiences in which Christian prayers were said aloud at the beginning of mandatory faculty gatherings. These teachers indicated a variety of reactions, including feeling that religion and state should remain separate, that their time was being wasted when they could be doing their teaching jobs, or that the worldviews of non-Christians were being marginalized as unimportant. None of these teachers protested openly, although they were disturbed by the obvious display of Christian privilege. It appeared to them that no one actually cared whether they participated in the prayer as long as they did not interrupt. Not feeling forced to participate played a critical role in their decisions not to protest.

All eleven participants noted that no one identifying as Jewish, Hindu, Buddhist, Muslim, or atheist offered a prayer or non-religious motivational comments at any of these faculty gatherings. The Christian privilege in this situation is all too obvious to non-Christian teachers. Margola (atheist/culturally Jewish) explained her feelings of marginalization during these experiences: "I'm thinking I'm just used to it. You just feel inundated with everything that's Jewish that doesn't belong. You knew you did not belong. You knew there wasn't a place for you."

Six participants reported that they had been in situations where Christian proselytizing took place at public school events. Here are three such reports. Andrea (atheist) was present at a mandatory faculty meeting at which a Christian speaker gave a "motivational" speech using the story of David and Goliath. In this speech, Christianity was directly advocated as the key to overcoming the challenges that the public school faculty would face during the upcoming school year. Andrea chose to temporarily remove herself from the auditorium: "At one point, I went into the bathroom, and I realized it was the club of women who just couldn't take it anymore, who decided to hide out in the bathroom."

Hannah (agnostic/culturally Jewish) attended a teacher-mandatory kick-off for the schools in her cluster at an evangelical megachurch. While Hannah observed church members approaching school participants to ask them to pray with them, what she found most off-putting about this event was the showing of a Christian video as an integral segment of the welcoming and motivational speeches given by school officials to the entire group of attendees. When Hannah brought up her concern with her fellow teachers later and "kind of got just a shrug off, eye-roll attitude about it," she was left to wonder if they supported the Christian proselytizing that had taken place at this school function. She felt uncomfortable and too vulnerable as a non-Christian in the majority Christian faculty to protest the Christian privilege displayed at this public school event.

Buddhist Fumiko's high school routinely rented a nearby Christian church to administer high-stakes standardized exams due to space constraints at the school. Fumiko noticed that "people from the church would try to talk to students as they were coming into tests and as they were leaving," and her students told her that the church members were offering to pray with them. Deeply concerned, Fumiko dashed off anonymous letters to the local newspaper, the school board of Central County, the principal, and even national groups for religious equity. While Fumiko has no idea if her anonymous letters were helpful in correcting this situation, she was not the only angry stakeholder. Local news reported that a parent complained to the administration, and that the administration requested that the church members discontinue the practice.[6] The church members ignored this request, showing up to invite students to pray as they entered the church building for testing the following day. Fumiko reported that the school no longer uses the facilities at this Christian church for school functions, although functions for the public high school are still held at other Christian churches.

The proselytizing experiences above involved participants as they took part in public school events either at the school itself or hosted by local Christian churches. These proselytizing events were not directed specifically at individual teachers but worked to produce an environment that privileged Christianity and marginalized non-Christians. It is telling that none of the participants felt that they could object to these proselytizing situations with anything more forceful than an anonymous letter written to a principal, county school board, or local newspaper. Is Christian privilege so firmly entrenched in some public schools in north Georgia that a non-Christian teacher openly requesting that religion and state remain separate might face unpleasant professional or personal consequences? The teacher participants were not willing to risk their jobs or reputations in the public schools to find out.

Participants of faith delicately navigate the stream of Christian privilege to be able to participate in their own non-Christian holidays and worship schedules. All participants of faith mentioned that the counties in which they worked allowed them to use three of their personal days to observe religious holidays. These three days are not added on to their personal days; they have the same number of personal days as Christian teachers whose religious observations are automatically accommodated by the school calendar. Aron (atheist/culturally Jewish), a teacher who reported that he chooses not to take Jewish holidays off, was nonetheless concerned: "I would have to take personal leave days, and I don't think that's ethical. It shouldn't cost me anything, so I do have a problem with that." Hannah (agnostic/culturally Jewish) also said that she rarely took time off for religious observances because she feels responsible for teaching the students who still attend school on those days. Bisma, who chooses not to outwardly identify as Muslim at the public middle school where she works, does request religious leave to celebrate Eid-al-Fitr, the three-day feast of thanksgiving at the end of Ramadan. However, she will "take a half-day off and come in later," rather than taking the full three days.

Matilda reported that asking her elementary school supervisor for time off to attend Jewish celebrations was an unpleasant task. She explained, "I can tell you that I was shocked when I got to the public schools at the backlash I got when the Jewish holidays came up. When I asked to take off, it was, 'Are you sure? Is it that important of a holiday that you need to take off?'" Matilda was required to find her own substitute for the three days of holiday leave she was grudgingly allowed as well as pay for the time off with her own personal days. Christians, with their holidays "naturally" worked into the school calendar, do not have to fight to ensure that they have the time to worship with their families on their religious holidays.

Margola (atheist/culturally Jewish) noted that three days of religious leave were not always sufficient to accommodate her participation in the most important Jewish holidays. She explained that she wanted to spend Yom Kippur with her family who lived a three-hour drive away, but because the observation began on a Tuesday night as based on the Hebrew calendar, she would have needed another half day of religious leave. She did not observe Yom Kippur with her family, concluding, "I have to make compromises because I've got work." Bina (Jewish) admitted that she does not make it to her synagogue when she has trouble leaving school early enough on Friday. She also finds herself in the uncomfortable position of having to explain that she cannot attend Friday evening or Saturday school activities because of her religious commitments. She observed, "[Administrators] understand why you can't be there, but you still have to say why." Vidula, a Hindu immigrant from India, was a bit disturbed by the (in)sensitivity of the American people to non-Christian religious holidays. She observed, "In India, it's like a mix of everybody and those public holidays are for everybody." To her, simply being obligated to request religious leave demonstrates to her that her religious observations are considered less important than Christian holidays here, which are automatically accommodated.

Nuha's religious needs were the only ones liberally accommodated by her administration. Friday, the Muslim sacred day of worship, is also a full official workday for public school teachers in the United States, which makes attending a worship service at a mosque at the traditional noon hour very challenging. However, the school arranges her schedule so that she is free to leave early every Friday and is not required to take personal leave for this time. This is an extraordinary religious accommodation that does not seem to be offered to others. However, while she appreciates the accommodations, she is never sure that new leadership at the school will continue to offer them. Ultimately, only Christian holidays and worship schedules are fully accommodated without teachers having to request time off, using one of their personal days in order to be paid, or being asked to justify why they cannot attend a Friday evening or Saturday school activity for religious purposes. School activities are not regularly (ever?) scheduled for Sunday mornings when most Christian services are held.

Ten non-Christian public school teacher participants found that dealing with the Christian theological certainty of others was problematic. All worked in schools in which the faculty and administration were majority Christian, although the students in these schools were religiously diverse. These teachers reported that Christian certainty presented in such ways as a Christian colleague harassing a transgender student or refusing to teach evolution even though it was in the curriculum; students refusing to learn the science of evolution because they believed it conflicted with their religious beliefs; and even a school board member suggesting to county science teachers that they should teach creationism or intelligent design along with evolution. These experiences made it difficult for the non-Christian participants to work with their theologically-certain Christian colleagues and for the biology teachers, especially, to teach evolutionary science to their theologically-certain students.

My study of non-Christian teachers confirms that Christian privilege is present in some north Georgia public schools. All of my sixteen non-Christian teacher interviewees recounted experiences they had with respect to Christian privilege that made them feel marginalized. These experiences influenced how they formed (or chose not to form) interpersonal relationships with colleagues and students. These non-Christian teachers made decisions about their professional lives based on the strength of the Christian privilege they perceived in the cultures of their public school workplaces and on a fear of losing the support of Christian supervisors. They felt that the Christian-privileged school culture silenced their voices and their worldviews. Are we powerless to change this?

Public schools are potentially ideal places to begin the process of making our communities more religiously plural. To a large extent, the issues of Christian privilege that this study found arose from an ignorance among administrators and faculty of First Amendment issues and religious diversity in general. A remedy for this could be administrator and faculty instruction in both the Establishment and the Free

Exercise clauses of the First Amendment. Comparative religious studies could also increase empathy among faculty and students. Since administrators set the tone for the faculty, their participation in the training is crucial. The situation is not hopeless, but a lot depends on the political climate outside the schools.

## FOR REFLECTION

1　What are some consequences of non-Christian teachers feeling that their voices are unwelcome in public school workspaces?

2　How might the exclusion of non-Christian teachers' worldviews affect the education offered to diverse religious students in the public schools?

3　How could a religiously diverse faculty work together more effectively to provide a high-quality education for all students?

# NOTES

1. See Warren J. Blumenfeld, "Christian Privilege and the Promotion of 'Secular' and Not-so 'Secular' Mainline Christianity in Public Schooling and in the Larger Society," *Equity & Excellence in Education* 39, no. 3 (2006): 195–210. See also Warren J. Blumenfeld, "Christian Privilege in the United States: An Overview," in *Investigating Christian Privilege and Religious Oppression in the United States*, eds. W. J. Blumenfeld, K. Y. Joshi, and E. E. Fairchild (Rotterdam: Sense Publishers, 2009), 3–22. See also Jason Nelson, "Christian Teachers and Christian Privilege," in *Investigating Christian Privilege and Religious Oppression in the United States*, 135–50.

2. Khyati Y. Joshi, *White Christian Privilege: The Illusion of Religious Equality in America* (New York: New York University Press, 2020), 21.

3. Vicki Scullion, "Non-Christian Teachers and Christian Privilege in Public Schools," Doctoral Dissertation, University of Georgia, 2022.

4. Several of the atheist or agnostic teachers came from a Christian background but, since they did not self-identify as "atheist/culturally Christian," they were accepted as study participants.

5. The names of all participants and identifying locations are pseudonyms used to protect their privacy.

6. Charles C. Haynes, "When Schools Go to Church, Conflict Follows." Freedom Forum Institute. May 23, 2011. https://www.freedomforuminstitute.org/.

# Part III

# Religiously Affiliated
## School Settings

# 10

# WITH UNAPOLOGETIC HUMILITY
### Why it is important for religious schools to commit to interreligious learning and dialogue

*Brendan O'Kane*

*The Church, therefore, exhorts her sons, that through dialogue and collaboration with the followers of other religions, carried out with prudence and love and in witness to the Christian faith and life, they recognize, preserve and promote the good things, spiritual and moral, as well as the socio-cultural values found among these men.*[1]

My experience in education has solely been in Catholic schools. Over the years, I have grown in my understanding of the fact that within Catholic teaching on religious, secondary education, there is an appreciation and affirmation of interreligious dialogue and learning. The quote above, from *Nostra aetate*, proclaimed in 1965, makes it clear that this needs to be a priority for all and is part of what it means to be Catholic. This appreciation and affirmation have been central in my development and belief that this focus is essential for all religious schools.

Parents and guardians want the best for their children. When it comes to choosing schools, religious schools have a unique appeal and are seen as the place their child can receive an education that goes beyond academics and extracurricular activities. It is an education that engages the soul. In an ever-changing world that beckons us to develop prowess in STEM (Science, Technology, Engineering, and Mathematics), a global perspective, and the ability to interact in a diverse world of people from various belief systems and backgrounds, it is essential religious schools recognize the importance of interreligious learning and dialogue. Attempts to broaden horizons and cultivate skills for navigating various landscapes might lead to some challenges. Despite these, it is necessary to persevere. Some might think these efforts will in some way jeopardize the authenticity of the school's founding principles or take it in a direction that is not faithful to the principles. These are real concerns that need to be addressed. However, the best way to do so is not to apologize or defend, but to proceed with humility, a dedication to realizing there is room to grow. Acknowledging the importance of interreligious learning does not necessarily lead to abandoning the mission and identity of the school.

So, how do we stay true to our mission and identity as a religious school and simultaneously prepare students for the world? How are we equipping students with the skills, empathy, and ability to learn from people in a way their own faith doesn't feel threatened, but gives the opportunity to grow from the interactions and become a fuller person in the world? These are some of the questions that invite all religious schools to further examination and growth, and thankfully the answers to many exist in the foundation and guiding texts of respective traditions.

## "Go Forth and Set the World on Fire"

When a child is sent to a school with a religious affiliation, even if it is not the primary reason that a  family has sent their children to such a school, it is safe to say the family expects education and experiences within that tradition. For us here at Loyola Blakefield, a Jesuit school, our mission and identity call us to a deepening in the Catholic faith—hence, to pay attention to and embrace direction from the Society of Jesus, also known as the Jesuits. We prepare students to "go forth and set the world on fire," as the Ignatian call states. They must lead with a strong foundation and an open heart, paying attention to where God is calling them. They are challenged to go forth and develop as global citizens. We inherit this disposition from our founder, Ignatius of Loyola, who was born in 1491 and is described by Jesuit historian Fr. John O'Malley, SJ as being a "worldly saint."[2] Ignatius is well known for his journey as a pilgrim. However, he spent an even greater amount of his time behind a desk, writing letters to his "friends in the Lord" and engaging in strategic planning for the Society of Jesus. According to José Mesa, SJ, Secretary for Secondary and Pre-Secondary Education, Society of Jesus:

> The Global dimension has always been part of the mission of the
> Society of Jesus. From the beginning, in the 1500's, St. Ignatius

and his fellow missionaries traveled the world, wrote letters to each other speaking about the experiences they were having, and the schools learned more about the world around them. Although our world has changed, this aspect of our mission has not. Arguably, it is more important now than ever, as we live in an increasingly interconnected world.[3]

Loyola Blakefield, located in Towson, Maryland is part of the Jesuit Global Network of Schools. In 1548, the first Jesuit school was founded in Messina, Italy. O'Malley states that Ignatius described Jesuit schools as works of charity, a contribution to what he called the "common good." Although being schoolteachers was not in the original plan for the Society of Jesus, it became the focus. According to the Jesuits,

> Today we count more than 2,300 schools in the Jesuit network in partnership between the Jesuit schools and a number of companion schools. Together we educate more than two million students, from all kinds of religious, cultural, social and language backgrounds in five continents and more than 70 countries.[4]

The Society of Jesus is constantly looking for ways to respond to the need for high quality education as evidenced in their efforts; these include creative models such as the Fe y Alegría network. According to UNICEF, over one billion children will head to school today and an estimated 617 million children and adolescents are unable to reach minimum proficiency levels in reading and mathematics, despite two thirds of them being in school. Magis Americas reports that in 2017 over 263 million children and youth around the world are still unable to attend school. The need is greater than ever and as Jesuit schools continue to expand, an emphasis on developing as a global citizen is essential.[5]

## INVITATION TO PROGRESS

In our local context, the first step for us was embracing our mission and looking at our religious identity as an invitation to continued progress. Our Catholic identity is an enabling vision and thus not an exclusionary one. Like our founder Ignatius, we commit to asking God to help us discern the signs of the times and work collaboratively. The Society of Jesus has been providing guidance and has shared the fruits of their discernment for hundreds of years. This has been a big reason why the educational network has been able to expand and maintain a unique identity with a common foundation. As a recent document entitled *Jesuit Schools: A Living Tradition* explains, Jesuit schools are committed to:

- Providing in-depth Catholic faith formation in dialogue with other religions and worldviews
- Creating a Safe and Healthy Environment for all
- Global Citizenship
- The Care of all Creation
- Justice
- Being Accessible for All
- Interculturality
- Being a Global Network at the service of the Mission
- Human Excellence
- Life-Long Learning

The goal of Ignatian Spirituality is "finding God in all things." With this effort as our main focus, combined with clear guidance and prioritization, we can work toward that goal in a way that embraces the global diversity of people, tradition, thought, and experiences in the world. According to the first point on this list of characteristics, we are being invited to engage in the work of interreligious education and dialogue. This work complements a robust educational curriculum and helps to prepare students to engage fully in the human experience.

## COMMITMENT

One of the greatest gifts of being in Towson, Maryland has been our proximity to the Institute for Islamic, Christian, and Jewish Studies (ICJS). In responding to the call to animate our mission, we realized that our faculty and staff needed to model how to do this in their commitment to interreligious education and dialogue. In recent years, faculty and staff have attended ICJS professional development, participated in the ICJS teachers fellowship program, and benefited greatly from the experience and expertise of ICJS scholars. With six educators who have been part of the fellowship program, Loyola Blakefield is better suited to journey with our youth as they develop and grow in their understanding of cultivating a deeper commitment to the importance of interreligious education and global citizenship.

Because of this collaboration, there have been highlights that illustrate what is possible when religious schools embrace a dedication to interreligious learning and dialogue. A transformative experience for us in 2019 was when Dr. Benjamin Sax spoke with our ninth-grade English students in relation to their classroom experience of reading *Maus: A Survivor's Tale,* a graphic novel by Art Spiegelman. Our students needed additional context, the opportunity to ask questions, and learn more about basic facts and differences from modern lived experience and the harmful power of stereotypes. As we now see this text in the news amidst discussions of banned books, it is more important to engage thoughtfully, with a focus on our mission and the end goal. A main reason for engaging in this lesson specifically can be found in the profile of *Graduate at Graduation*.[6] Originally published in 1980 and updated since then, student development in Jesuit schools has been informed by the Graduate at Graduation goals. Commonly referred to as the "Grad at Grad," all students are challenged to grow during their time with us in a variety of areas. Under the category, "committed to doing justice," it states, "By graduation the student already is developing, from reflection on experiences with the marginalized, a sense of compassion and a growing understanding of those social changes which will assist all in attaining their basic human rights." Now, in the time Dr. Sax had with our Dons, it was impossible to cover everything, but he journeyed with us to a better place—a place of greater understanding.

Also in 2019, we held a prayer service titled, "Thankful for my faith which calls me to...." Our teachers fellowship participants were able to reflect on their experience with the ICJS program and how it helped to illuminate the importance of addressing bias, blind spots, or simply what is missed when we do not take time to learn and listen. This is a sample of what two of our teachers had to say:[7]

> When asked, ICJS often repeated to us that the only goal of the program was to foster interfaith dialogue between educators so that we might better be able to enrich our students' experiences as a result of what we personally learned. Teaching in a Catholic school as a Christian who grew up in a Christian family and attended Catholic schools throughout my life, my interfaith experience has been somewhere between negligible and nonexistent. It was great to have the chance to speak with individuals of Muslim, Jewish, and even, in one case, Asatro faith traditions, [which] gave me opportunities to more appropriately and accurately answer student questions during study of Art Spiegelman's *Maus*, Neil Gaiman's Norse Mythology text, and even during our study of

contemporary American literature as a response to 9/11 and the Islamophobia that became a part of America at the time.

—*Brendan Bailey*

Religious literacy and the mindset that it creates facilitates the creation of solutions to common issues so that we can understand each other better rather than feel threatened by these differences. We can then develop the ability to evaluate issues of justice in a way that respects others beliefs. I believe that religious discussion is necessary in a true democracy as history has revealed what the consequences of religious intolerance can be.

—*Selma Ciccarone*

Modeling the importance of implementing newly found knowledge or information about how to be more respectful and inclusive, our adults communicated to our students that it is important to commit to lifelong learning.

Our teachers fellows have influenced our curriculum by prioritizing readings and course material that, anchored in our mission, calls students to expand their understanding of history and the world around them. They are also teachers who ask questions in meetings such as, "how can we be mindful of our non-Catholic students? What is their experience?" The lessons they have designed invite our students to a heightened sensitivity and spark an interest in learning more. An example lesson for this was created by one of our Theology teachers, Dan Knapp, who incorporates Rabbi Abraham Joshua Heschel and Rev. Dr. Martin Luther King Jr. when teaching his Prophets unit. An in-depth study of the context in which the two existed and the role religion played in their work and partnership presents a lesson where students can learn and witness to the power of interfaith collaboration.

We have teachers who are deeply committed to their own development. In addition to opportunities such as the ICJS teachers fellowship, they are active in their spiritual formation, professional development, and student life. One example of their dedication is the seventeen people in the last three years who have prayed the nineteenth annotation of the Spiritual Exercises, which has a daily prayer commitment of one hour in addition to weekly meetings with a spiritual director for nine months. This retreat is rooted in the Catholic faith and Ignatian spirituality and as I mentioned earlier, this is not a fact that should be diminished but is one of the main reasons why those who complete it are more open to answering the call to interreligious learning and dialogue. They are better able to look for and embrace "God in all things." We believe that people who take their faith seriously and make time for quiet discernment are inspired to respond to the needs of our community and of society as a whole.

## CHALLENGES

The challenges we have faced, as a religious school seeking to grow in interreligious learning and dialogue, have been invitations to think creatively about what it means to be committed to these efforts. For example, one of our challenges is gathering and prioritizing information from those who are not in the religious majority. Since we have a predominantly Catholic student body, faculty, and staff, when we seek input and guidance from those who are not Catholic, we need to consider the fact that people who are in the minority might not feel comfortable or empowered to share their beliefs openly. There also might be some hesitation in sharing a personal aspect when it might not be met with a shared or affirming experience.

As a result of learning through professional development and collaboration with other Jesuit schools, a few of the ways we have taken steps to address this include our implementation of the program, "Come Worship With Us," which offers faculty and staff the opportunity to invite people to come to their place of worship. In the planning stages of this program, I was able to attend a Baptist service for the first time, and since then I have been able to participate in services at six separate places of worship (often followed by a meal). I have witnessed my colleagues serve and read, and have grown in my admiration of them. One weekend a big group of us attended St. Matthew Catholic Church in Baltimore and I remember looking down the row, seeing fellow faculty and staff, many of us there for the first time, eager and willing to pray and learn together. Ultimately, we would like to get to the point where all people feel comfortable inviting a small group of people to pray with them.

In our first year, the "Come Worship With Us" program was well received. Although the places we visited were still within the Christian tradition, there was more exposure and an opportunity for authentic sharing. We plan to expand this to visiting non-Christian places of worship. We took another proactive step this past year and our Director of Campus Ministry, Laura McCormack, organized a prayer service focused on Christian unity. In participating in the International Week of Prayer for Christian Unity, we realized there is a great need to focus on how Christians are relating with other Christians. When we are better able to notice, learn, and celebrate other Christians we will be better served when widening that circle. We view this as an essential step that will strengthen any subsequent efforts made in interreligious learning and dialogue.

## CONCLUSION

Again, parents and guardians want the best for their children. If they send them to a religious school, the definition of "the best" has evolved to include preparing them for the diverse world outside the school walls. Religious schools should feel confident in leading with their mission and identity, anchoring any steps taken to embrace interreligious learning and dialogue in this foundation. Specifically in our context, this call has been laid out for us by the Jesuits. If your school is not in the same position, then it is time to go back to the beginning—to the roots of why the school was founded—and spend time discerning the signs of the times and how to best journey with our youth in our current context. If we are all paying attention to trends and the changing world, the need for a focus on interreligious learning and dialogue is undeniable. We have decided an essential part of this process is the faculty and staff that spend hours a day with our youth, and we realized it cannot simply be our Theology department. It takes an institutional commitment, which begins by recognizing the need and the call.

In conversations with members of our community, when asked about how we do this, we have learned one common way of proceeding that is noticed and felt is the focus on hospitality. One community member shared that, despite her husband not being Catholic, they feel comfortable and appreciated. This is important for us because diversity makes us all better. For someone who is not in the religious majority to feel safe and valued takes extra effort on their part already. We need to recognize this and make sure we're also taking steps and prioritizing their experience.

Our future requires an openness and a willingness to learn and grow. Just as we know that the classes, programs, or prayer services we offer are not covering all aspects, we offer them as an entryway, a launching point for what is hopefully a life filled with the desire to learn more and grow in the love of God and neighbor, which is the ultimate end of our work as stated by Pope Paul VI in *Nostra aetate*:

> We cannot truly call on God, the Father of all, if we refuse to treat in a brotherly way any man, created as he is in the image of God. Man's relation to God the Father and his relation to men his brothers are so linked together that Scripture says: "He who does not love does not know God" (1 John 4:8).[8]

## FOR REFLECTION

1  How did your educational experience prepare you to interact with and appreciate people who might not share the same religious tradition as you?

2  How does St. Ignatius of Loyola's invitation to find God in all things expand your motivation to engage in interreligious learning and dialogue?

3  How else do you think religious schools need to adapt to provide a high-quality educational experience for students?

# NOTES

1. For the full text of *Nostra aetate,* see the online archive at www.vatican.va.

2. John W. O'Malley , S. J., "How the First Jesuits Became Involved in Education" in Vincent Duminuco, ed., *The Jesuit Ratio Studiorum: 400th Anniversary Perspectives* (New York: Fordham University Press, 2000).

3. "Global Citizenship—Ignatian Context," *educate magis*, (November 26, 2019).

4. "Education," The Society of Jesus, www.jesuits.global/ministries/education/.

5. The Society of Jesus Secretariat for Education (Rome), www.educatemagis.org.

6. For a description, see Matt Emerson, "The 'Grad at Grad' and Jesuit Schools" in *America: The Jesuit Review* (May 21, 2014).

7. These teachers have given permission for the inclusion of their comments here, with attribution.

8. *Nostra aetate.*

# 11

# CRITICAL RELIGIOUSLY SUSTAINING PEDAGOGY
## A Framework of Theological Education for and with Non-Catholic Students in Catholic Secondary Schools

*David Michael Avram Gregory*

In the past half-century, the tone and timbre of Catholic education have shifted tremendously. Because of the constellation of perceived (and hopefully actual) qualities—such as rigorous discipline, loving community, and thorough academic preparation—that many families believe distinguish Catholic schools over and above their public counterparts, in recent decades Catholic schools have diversified across demographic categories. Racially, socioeconomically, and religiously diverse families send their children into the world of Catholic education for a variety of reasons.[1] Catholic schools no longer primarily serve ghettoized immigrant Catholic populations (as they did for the first century or so of their existence in the US), but rather open their doors to all who can afford to attend, be it through their own financial resources or through the help of scholarship opportunities. Catholic schools' revenues remain largely tuition-driven, causing many of them to become elitist, and causing urban Catholic schools to be frequent participants in socioeconomically- and racially-driven segregationist practices.[2]

In the early 1970s, non-Catholic students in Catholic high schools accounted for just over 2% of total enrollment; now they account for around 25%—and some schools' students are mostly non-Catholic.[3] This reality of Catholic schools' students' religious diversification poses an interesting question for the religious educators working in them: What should the goals of religious education (hereafter "RE") be for students who are non-Catholic, or not practicing any religious tradition whatsoever?

## THE PROBLEMS OF CATECHESIS AND THE *USCCB* FRAMEWORK

In 2008, the United States Conference of Catholic Bishops (henceforward the USCCB) published *Doctrinal Elements of a Curriculum Framework for the Development of Catechetical Materials for Young People of High School Age* (henceforward the *Framework*), which mandated a standard theology curriculum for use in all United States Catholic high schools and parish youth ministry programs.[4] Perhaps intending to address increasing Catholic disaffiliation through a catechetical conveyance of Catholic doctrine, the bishops crafted their *Framework* to address this decline.

In their *Framework*, the bishops provided little more than a list of doctrinal and dogmatic items that they expect high school students to learn through theology coursework. Furthermore, the *Framework*'s catechetical formulation demonstrated the bishops' espousal of the "banking model" of education, which Freire had so vigorously critiqued in *Pedagogy of the Oppressed*.[5] While part of the bishops' role is to provide authoritative guidance in line with their magisterial authority (that is, their authority as ordained teachers of the faith), much of their understanding of a "correct" education has most likely been influenced by their own experiences of education. Non-catechetical models of religious education only became popular in the years following the Second Vatican Council. Thus, it is logical to infer that the bishops intended for their *Framework* to enforce catechesis because that is what they knew and understood in their own educational experiences. The *Framework*'s catechetical intent is, after all, stated outright in its full title, and it mirrors the structure of the *Catechism of the Catholic Church*.[6]

In crafting the *Framework* behind closed doors, the bishops did little to engage stakeholders, such as the hundreds of theology teachers, or the many thousands of students taking theology classes in Catholic schools around the United States.[7] Regarding their development of the *Framework*, I question whether the bishops have exercised their magisterial authority pastorally (that is, as empathetic and sympathetic shepherds of those faithful entrusted to their care), or even in accord with teachings published by the Vatican. After all, the Second Vatican Council's *Dignitatis humanae* articulated the immense value of a person's well-formed religious conscience and condemned any government intrusion into that particular freedom.[8] Given that catechizing those who do not seek catechesis is nothing less than a violation of religious freedom, the bishops of the USCCB contradicted the spirit of *Dignitatis Humanae*, whose authors attempted to foster interreligious and cross-cultural engagement. Hypothetically, the only context in which catechesis does not violate religious freedom would be one in which students, Catholic or otherwise, freely accept catechesis in full knowledge of its content and purposes. While non-Catholic families enroll their children in Catholic schools presumably understanding that Catholic theological education is an important aspect of the curriculum, one would only hope that such education is not coercive or insensitive to the religious beliefs of these students. This said, I suspect that sustaining the religious freedom of non-Catholic students was simply a negligible goal for the bishops, because they were primarily concerned with sustaining Catholic students' doctrinal literacy.

Ultimately, the bishops of the USCCB interpreted theological education as catechetical, and in so doing, employed the banking model of education in their crafting and mandating of the *Framework*. To apply Freire's thought, the bishops undertook "[c]ultural invasion, which serves the ends of conquest and the preservation of oppression," and "always involves a parochial view of reality, a static perception of the world, and the imposition of one world view upon another."[9] Moreover, the very nature of catechetical religious education, which potentially forces Catholic doctrine upon those who are not Catholic, or might not want it, "implies the 'superiority' of the invader and the 'inferiority' of those who are invaded, as well as the imposition of values by the former, who possess the latter and are afraid of losing them."[10] The USCCB's bishops approached theological education as something done *upon* students, rather than as a critical process of dialogue concerning the spiritual and religious dimensions of human existence.

Scholars and educators have questioned—for several decades, long before the *Framework* came into existence—whether the aforementioned catechetical mode of religious education effectively engages non-Catholics.[11] I believe that the *Framework* is not only ineffective at converting non-Catholics to Catholicism (because religious conversion entails far more than the learning of doctrine), but that it also systemically oppresses non-Catholic learners, both on religious and cultural levels. Ultimately, the US bishops, in attempting to catechize and deepen students' Catholicity through their *Framework*, fail to educate non-Catholics appropriately or respectfully, and do symbolic violence upon them through theological coercion. Although much of Catholic Social Teaching is liberating (for example, the preferential option for the poor, the dignity and rights of immigrants, and the long tradition of just wages and workers' rights), certain teachings might be traumatizing for students who identify as belonging to queer communities, or whose parents are divorced.

There are certainly theology teachers who agree with the bishops and would maintain that catechesis is the preferred mode of religious education for Catholic high schools. However, based on Vatican documents and evidence from extant scholarship, I argue that catechesis can only appropriately be applied to homogeneous Catholic student populations whose beliefs completely cohere with the full content of Catholic doctrinal and dogmatic teaching. In the words of Crawford and Rossiter, "No amount of religious education can generate faith or bring about committed participation in a parish."[12] In short, helping students become faithful Catholics requires more than catechetics, such as parental involvement or regular participation in a religious community.

In the words of the De La Salle Christian Brother Gerard Rummery (1975), who was among the first to critique the prospect of catechesis for religiously diverse students, "this kind of authoritative approach has little chance of leading towards personal faith as distinct from the social experience of faith" because the "very presumption of faith with many adolescent pupils in these circumstances, seems sufficient to alienate them."[13] Not only does catechesis alienate non-Catholic students, however, but it others, silences, negates, degrades, oppresses, and invisibilizes their religious and spiritual cultures and beliefs.[14] A number of documents from the bishops of Congregation for Catholic Education (henceforward the "CCE") have acknowledged the shifting nature of Catholic schools' students' religious demographics across the globe, and the CCE's bishops and cardinals have posited that religious education need not be catechetical.[15] In the introduction to *The Religious Dimension of Education in the Catholic School*, for example, Cardinal William Baum wrote of non-Catholic students' presence in Catholic schools:

> The religious freedom and the personal conscience of individual students and their families must be respected, and this freedom is explicitly recognized by the Church. On the other hand, a Catholic school cannot relinquish its own freedom to proclaim the Gospel and to offer a formation based on the values to be found in a Christian education; this is its right and its duty. To proclaim or to offer is not to impose, however; the latter suggests a moral violence which is strictly forbidden, both by the Gospel and by Church law.[16]

Baum believed that infringing upon the religious consciences of non-Catholic students would be an act of symbolic moral violence. The bishops of the USCCB failed to echo the safeguarding of personal conscience and religious freedom in any of their documents pertaining to education.

## CRITICAL RELIGIOUSLY SUSTAINING PEDAGOGY

In light of the profound disservice that catechetical education does to religiously diverse students in Catholic high schools, I propose an alternative framework of religious education for such contexts: Critical Religiously Sustaining Pedagogy (henceforward "CRSP"). CRSP synthesizes several strands of critical pedagogy, all of which descend from Freire's revolutionary theories.[17] Freire's central concept of *conscientização,* or the awakening and raising of consciousness, is geared toward praxis, or "*critical intervention* in reality."[18] Emancipatory education invites students to critically interrogate their lives, and the worlds they inhabit, in order to catalyze action in the battle against the death-dealing forces that ripple throughout and undergird systemic injustice.

A number of critical theorists and practitioners have all grounded their work in Freire's insights. Ladson-Billings's development of Culturally Relevant Pedagogy is "specifically committed to collective, not merely individual, empowerment."[19] In her pursuit of working for collective student empowerment, Ladson-Billings argued that Culturally Relevant Pedagogy helps every student experience academic success, engage culturally competent practices, and develop a critical consciousness through which they can challenge hegemonic, systemic forces in culture and society. Gay's work on multicultural education led her to develop Culturally Responsive Teaching, which "acknowledges the legitimacy of cultural heritages," influences how students learn, and what content they might want to learn. It "builds bridges of meaningfulness between home and school experiences" and "between academic abstractions and lived sociocultural realities." It "uses a wide variety of instructional strategies" so as to accommodate each and every learner; "teaches students to know and praise their own and one another's cultural heritages," which characterizes asset-based pedagogies; and "incorporates multicultural information, resources and materials in all the subjects and skills."[20] Even though Gay and Ladson-Billings did not address religious education, I assert that catechetical religious education is an example of the hegemonically-oriented pedagogy that Gay and Ladson-Billings critiqued. Catechesis acknowledges the legitimacy of only one religious tradition, fails to develop bridges of meaning between students' learning and life worlds, and approaches non-Catholic religious traditions through a deficit lens.

Culturally Sustaining Pedagogy pushed the extant bounds of Culturally Relevant Pedagogy and Culturally Responsive Teaching.[21] Pioneers Paris and Alim wrote that, "Instead of being oppressive, homogenizing forces, Culturally Sustaining Pedagogy asks us to reimagine schools as sites where diverse, heterogeneous practices are not only valued but sustained," and therefore "demands a critical, emancipatory vision of schooling that reframes the object of critique from our children to oppressive systems."[22] From a starting point of asset-based (rather than deficit-based) pedagogy, practitioners of Culturally Sustaining Pedagogy leverage students' skills alongside their cultural and linguistic funds of knowledge, while recognizing that these resources are fluid, dynamically coexisting, and moving between cultural worlds. The Catholic tradition has long incorporated an awareness of social and structural sin into its moral theologies, and Culturally Sustaining Pedagogy shares a very similar awareness.

Finally, for the past fifteen or so years, Andrew Wright in the U.K. has been the pioneering advocate for the still-developing theoretical and pedagogical model that he calls "Critical Religious Education."[23] Wright bases Critical Religious Education on the perspective that we "have a moral obligation to seek to hold true beliefs" and the assumption that society will flourish if citizens can "respond intelligently to questions about the ultimate meaning and purpose of life."[24] As the authors of the 2019 handbook of Critical Religious Education stated, it is "the only approach to RE which has explicitly forwarded a non-confessional realist approach over the last two decades."[25] Given its philosophical grounding, Critical Religious Education provides a helpful lens with which one can engage questions and goals regarding authentic religious exploration in a theology classroom.

Combining elements from each of these critical pedagogies, I have created the framework of Critical Religiously Sustaining Pedagogy (Figure 1). This framework is predicated upon the overarching goals of Freirean emancipatory education and the Catholic educational mission of evangelization, which surround CRSP's three fundamental tenets: religiously sustaining instruction; nurturing and loving relationships; and existentially meaningful (that is, meaningful to students' lived experiences) content.

The universal mission of Catholic education centralizes evangelization, as articulated by the CCE. I presently employ "evangelization" not in the sense of attempting the conversion of non-Catholics to Catholicism, but rather in terms of theology teachers living out their faiths and teaching their students while grounded in faith-filled love of Jesus, thereby striving to actualize the mission of Catholic schools to embody the Gospel message. In this, I sympathize with Pope Francis, who in his apostolic exhortation *Evangelii gaudium* wrote: "Instead of seeming to impose new obligations, [Catholics] should appear as people who wish to share their joy, who point to a horizon of beauty and who invite others to a delicious banquet. It is not by proselytizing that the Church grows, but 'by attraction.'"[26] Throughout his exhortation, Francis called for Catholics to consider new and creative means of evangelization, apart from the transmission of doctrine, so as to combat wicked forces such as the idolatry of money, the disposability of the human person, and injustices that spawn violence. Freirean emancipatory education provides a more focused foundation for CRSP to rest on: Freire's tenets of praxis-oriented conscientization, problem-posing and constructive dialogue, and humanizing relationships echo throughout CRSP's elemental tenets.

CRSP's three tenets are based upon elements from the theories of Culturally Relevant Pedagogy, Culturally Responsive Teaching, Culturally Sustaining Pedagogy, and Critical Religious Education. By existentially meaningful content, I refer to the curricular content in theology classes, particularly with regard to whether or not it helps students to understand their beliefs, the beliefs of those in their immediate communities, and the ways in which religious dynamics influence culture and society. Hence, even if a student does not possess or seek to possess any form of religious belief, the study of theology can still possess immense relevance in pursuit of reading the world around them, to cast this notion in Freirean language. The goal of pursuing existentially meaningful content is starkly opposed to the goals of catechetical religious education, which is not necessarily relevant for the lived experience of teenagers. Just as Critical Relevant Pedagogy and Critical Relevant Teaching approached students as persons in need of culturally responsive and relevant engagement, and Culturally Sustaining Pedagogy approached student cultures as fluid, theological education

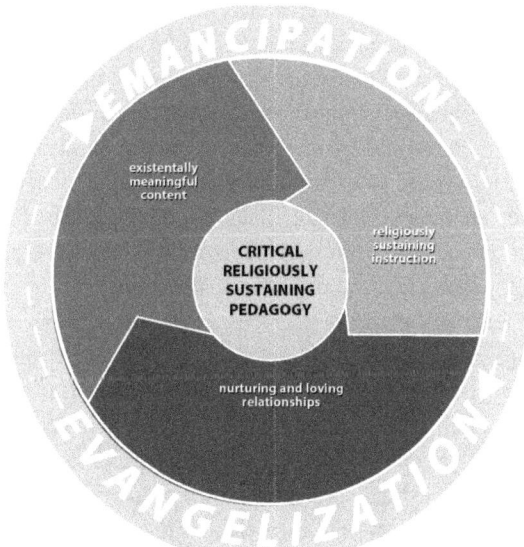

**FIGURE 1: CRITICAL RELIGIOUSLY
SUSTAINING PEDAGOGY**

that is sensitive to students' religious diversity can approach their religious and non-religious beliefs in a similar manner.

Religiously sustaining instruction refers to the means in and through which theology teachers engage students with the content of a given theology class, and how they invite students to express and interrogate their religious beliefs through this instruction. Regardless of what religious tradition or atheistic or agnostic beliefs a student ascribes to, religiously sustaining theological education can help students understand why they believe what they believe. I view this humanizing work as parallel to what Paris and Alim prioritized in Culturally Sustaining Pedagogy, because religiously sustaining theological education would not negate, silence, or oppress non-Catholic beliefs, but rather help a non-Catholic student to define those beliefs, which can be accomplished either through dialogue or reflective elements within a curriculum. By "religious," I do not necessarily mean that which belongs to organized religion, but rather that which belongs to questions of religious and spiritual significance more broadly: the existence of God, the immortality of the soul, the meaning of human existence, the exploration of good and evil, so on and so forth. While this is by no means an exhaustive list of themes that occur in all religious traditions, I paint with broad brushstrokes to articulate that which undergirds theological education in the Catholic tradition. Paul Griffiths has defined the "religious account" to be the interpretive framework through which a person makes sense of their phenomenal experience of the world, and is comprehensive, unsurpassable, and central; whether or not one ascribes to a religious tradition or not, every individual holds an implicit religious account, through which all their experiences and understandings are filtered.[27] Certainly, an authentically sustaining theological education would consider the questions that students themselves raise. Encouraging students' voices can enable them to understand their beliefs, and learn to communicate them in a democratic and religiously diverse society, as well as engage the beliefs of others with understanding and compassion.

Finally, the tenet of nurturing and loving relationships refers to the learning relationships that teachers foster, and how teachers learn about and engage students, regardless of what beliefs students hold. Any high-quality educator understands that their students learn best in the context of authentic relationships. Many first-year teachers are exposed to the pithy maxim "they don't care about what you know until they know that you care," which does indeed contain an immense amount of truth.[28] Just as the potential barriers erected by racial, ethnic, and cultural tensions can be dissolved through authentic love (precisely because that love challenges systemic injustice), so too can relationships overcome potential educational challenges caused by religious difference. I do not posit the import of authentic love in a romanticized or an idealized way. Informed by Freire's emphasis on the presence of hope in emancipatory education, I recognize that authentic love confronts injustice and interrupts and battles to overcome systemic oppression, even in the face of futility.[29] The centrality of relationships between educators and students resonates throughout the theoretical frameworks of Culturally Relevant Pedagogy, Culturally Relevant Teaching, and Culturally Sustaining Pedagogy, and so I take up this mantra in CRSP.

These three tenets feed into one another, support one another, draw from one another, and depend on one another. For example, a critical religiously sustaining pedagogy fosters nurturing and loving relationships between teacher and student through mutual self-revelation, which is to say the sharing of personal beliefs and the ensuing dialogue about them. The teacher demonstrates their care for the student by respecting their beliefs, perhaps even amplifying those beliefs, and thereby uplifting the student's dignity and reverencing the student's positionality. This, in turn, motivates the teacher to pursue existentially meaningful instruction that generates constant connections between the student's lived experience and the theological content of study. For example, in my own classroom of the past six years, wherein over 90% of my students identified as people of color, I taught the Hebrew Bible's prophetic literature by means of an intertextual engagement with hip-hop music; we read each prophet alongside a curated playlist—developed by students over the years—of contemporary artists such as Tupac, Lauryn Hill, Calle 13, Ana Tijoux, and Chance the Rapper. The unit concluded with a creative project around people whom students believed to be prophetic, either religious or otherwise; in all assignments, I gave students the freedom to express their own religious and political views, so long as they did so in critical engagement with scriptural texts.

Theology teachers would greatly benefit from leaning into, and learning from, critical pedagogies such as Culturally Responsive Pedagogy, Culturally Relevant Teaching, Culturally Sustaining Pedagogy, and Critical Religious Education. Broader educational scholarship tends to ignore religious beliefs as a central dimension of human culture, focusing on spoken and written language and collaborative learning styles. Teachers in many schools go through professional development that exposes them to means of creating more inclusive and welcoming classrooms that strive to guarantee the success of all students. Students of many different religious backgrounds (or none whatsoever) are now taking theology classes in Catholic high schools, and student populations will continue to diversify with respect to their religious affiliations. If we can collectively transition the paradigm of culturally relevant, responsive, and sustaining pedagogy towards religiously relevant, responsive, and sustaining pedagogy, I believe that such an effort would benefit theology teachers immensely.

Kinloch stated that "for CSP to be effective, then collaborative, collective, critical, and loving environments must be fostered that support young people's cultural identities," and in order to do so,

> we must work to combat and eradicate oppressive, racist educational policies that advantage monoculturalism, that debase the linguistic virtuosities of communities of color, and that recode terms such as *relevance* and *responsiveness* to mark tolerance over acceptance, normalization over difference, demonization over humanization, and hate over love.[30]

If we replace "racist" with "hegemonically Catholic," "monoculturalism" with "monoreligiosity," "linguistic virtuosities" with "religious virtuosities," and "communities of color" with "non-Catholic communities," we arrive at a perspective of Culturally Sustaining Pedagogy that foregrounds the role of religion in students' cultures. While religious education remains largely anathema to public education in the US (although certain IB and humanities programs involve education about religion in their curricula), students will continue to bring their beliefs into the classroom, unspoken though they may be. If non-Catholic students continue to matriculate into Catholic high schools in increasing numbers, and if Catholic students become less and less invested in their inherited religious tradition, theology teachers will have much to learn from these many strands of critical pedagogy and will do well to reassess the appropriateness of catechesis and the USCCB *Framework* in their teaching.

## FOR REFLECTION

1   What aspects of catechetical education need to be discarded for the religious education of non-Catholic students in Catholic high schools? What aspects can be "translated" for the sake of relevance and building bridges to the lived experiences of students?

2   Now that the USCCB *Framework* has been around for over a decade, is there room to re-think its appropriateness, as defined and understood by educators teaching across a wide variety of Catholic high schools?

3   In what ways can schools, theology departments, and theology teachers rebel against the catechetical strictures of the USCCB *Framework*? Are these agents already ignoring, diverging from, or rebelling against the *Framework*? If so, how so?

# NOTES

1. See Eric R. Eide, Dan D. Goldhaber, and Mark H. Showalter, "Does Catholic High School Attendance Lead to Attendance at a More Selective College?" *Social Science Quarterly* 85, no. 5 (2004): 1335–52. See also, David J. Fleming, Stéphane Lavertu, and William Crawford, "High School Options and Post-Secondary Student Success: The Catholic School Advantage," *Journal of Catholic Education* 21, no. 2 (2018): 1–25; Maureen T. Hallinan and Warren N. Kubitschek, "School Sector, School Poverty, and the Catholic School Advantage," *Journal of Catholic Education* 14, no. 2 (2013): 143–72; and Jennifer S. Maney, Carrie King, and Thomas J. Kiely, "Who Do You Say You Are: Relationships and Faith in Catholic Schools," *Journal of Catholic Education* 21, no. 1 (2017): 36–61.

2. Kevin J. Burke and Brian R. Gilbert, "Racing Tradition: Catholic Schooling and the Maintenance of Boundaries," *Race Ethnicity and Education* 19, no. 3 (2016): 524–45.

3. Dale McDonald and Margaret M. Schultz, *United States Catholic Elementary and Secondary Schools 2020–2021: The Annual Statistical Report on Schools, Enrollment and Staffing* (Leesburg, VA: National Catholic Education Association, 2021).

4. *United States Conference of Catholic Bishops, Doctrinal Elements of a Curriculum Framework for the Development of Catechetical Materials for Young People of High School Age* (Washington, DC: USCCB, 2008). To understand the shifting demographics of students in Catholic high schools, one need only look at any number of reports from the Pew Research Center to track the continuing decline of those who identify as Catholic. For extraordinary research on the religious identities of twenty-first century teenagers, see Christian Smith and Melinda Lundquist Denton, *Soul Searching: The Religious and Spiritual Lives of American Teenagers* (Oxford: University of Oxford Press, 2009), 74.

5. Paulo Freire, trans. Myra Bergman Ramos, *Pedagogy of the Oppressed: 50th Anniversary Edition* (1970; reis., London: Bloomsbury Academic, 2018).

6. Catholic Church, *Catechism of the Catholic Church: Revised in Accordance with the Official Latin Text Promulgated by Pope John Paul II* (1992; reis., Washington, DC: United States Catholic Conference, 1997).

7. John O'Malley, "Faulty Guidance: A New Framework for High School Catechesis Fails to Persuade," www.americamagazine.org; Carrie J. Schroeder, "The USCCB Curriculum Framework: Origins, Questions, and a Call for Research," *Journal of Catholic Education* 19, no. 1 (2015): 5–26.

8. Pope Paul VI, "Dignitatis humanae: Declaration on Religious Freedom on the Right of the Person and of Communities to Social and Civil Freedom in Matters Religious," https://www.vatican.va/archive.

9. Freire, *Pedagogy of the Oppressed*, 160.

10. Freire, *Pedagogy of the Oppressed*, 160.

11. See Thomas H. Groome, *Christian Religious Education: Sharing Our Story and Vision* (San Francisco: Harper and Row, 1980). See also, Thomas H. Groome, *Will There Be Faith? A New Vision for Educating and Growing Disciples* (New York: HarperOne, 2011); Maria Harris and Gabriel Moran, "Catechetical Language and Religious Education," *Theology Today* 49, no. 1 (1992): 21–30; Maria Harris and Gabriel Moran, *Reshaping Religious Education: Conversations on Contemporary Practice* (Louisville, KY: Westminster John Knox Press, 1988); Gabriel Moran, *Religious Education Development: Images for the Future* (Minneapolis, MN: Winston Press, 1983); Gabriel Moran, *Religious Education as a Second Language* (Birmingham, AL: Religious Education Press, 1989); Gabriel Moran, *Showing How: The Act of Teaching* (Valley Forge, PA: Trinity Press International, 1997); Gabriel Moran, *Missed Opportunities: Rethinking Catholic Tradition* (Bloomington, IN: Universe, 2016); Graham M. Rossiter, "The Need for a 'Creative Divorce' between Catechesis and Religious Education in Catholic Schools," *Religious Education* 77, no. 1 (1982): 21–40; Graham M. Rossiter, "Reorienting the Religion Curriculum in Catholic Schools to Address the Needs of Contemporary Youth Spirituality," *International Studies in Catholic Education* 3, no. 1 (2011): 57–72; Gerard Rummery, *Catechesis and Religious Education in a Pluralist Society* (Huntington, IN: Our Sunday Visitor, 1976); Daniel S. Schipani, *Religious Education Encounters Liberation Theology* (Birmingham, AL: Religious Education Press, 1988); John B. Switzer, "Strangers No More: The Pedagogy of Interreligious Hospitality," PhD diss., (Boston College, 2006); and Andrew Wright, *Critical Religious Education, Multiculturalism and the Pursuit of Truth* (Cardiff: University of Wales Press, 2007).

12.  Marisa Crawford and Graham Rossiter, *Reasons for Living: Education and Young People's Search for Meaning, Identity and Spirituality—A Handbook* (Victoria, Australia: Acer Press, 2006), 397.

13. Rummery, *Catechesis and Religious Education*, 168.

14. Regarding the damaging effects of indoctrinatory religious education, see Ursula S. Aldana, "'Does Jesus Want Us to Be Poor?' Student Perspectives of the Religious Program at a Cristo Rey Network School," *Journal of Catholic Education* 19, no. 1 (2015): 201–22. Brittany Aronson, Tasneem Amatullah, and Judson Laughter, "Culturally Relevant Education: Extending the Conversation to Religious Diversity," *Multicultural Perspectives* 18, no. 3

(2016): 140–49. Olaf Franck, "Critical Religious Education: Highlighting Religious Truth-Claims in Non-Confessional Educational Contexts," *British Journal of Religious Education* 37, no. 3 (2015): 225–39. Michael Hand, "The Problem with Faith Schools: A Reply to My Critics," *Theory and Research in Education* 2, no. 3 (2004): 343–53). Jack A. Hill, "Fighting the Elephant in the Room: Ethical Reflections on White Privilege and Other Systems of Advantage in the Teaching of Religion," *Teaching Theology & Religion* 12, no. 1 (2009): 3–23.

15. See Gabriel-Marie Garrone and the Congregation for Catholic Education, "The Catholic School," www.vatican.va, 1977; Pio Laghi, José Saraiva Martins, and the Congregation for Catholic Education, "The Catholic School on the Threshold of the Third Millennium," www.vatican.va, 1997; Zenon Grocholewski and the Congregation for Catholic Education, "Educating to Intercultural Dialogue in Catholic Schools: Living in Harmony for a Civilization of Love," www.vatican.va, 2013; The Congregation for Catholic Education, "Educating Today and Tomorrow: A Renewing Passion (Instrumentum Laboris)," www.vatican.va, 2014.

16. William Baum and the Congregation for Catholic Education, "The Religious Dimension of Education in the Catholic School," www.vatican.va, 1988.

17. Interestingly, Freire can be considered a founder of liberation theology, given that his praxis of emancipatory pedagogy influenced the development of Latin American liberation theology. See James D. Kirylo and Drick Boyd, Paulo Freire: *His Faith, Spirituality, and Theology* (Rotterdam: Sense Publishers, 2017).

18. Freire, *Pedagogy of the Oppressed*, 81, italics his.

19. Gloria Ladson-Billings, "But That's Just Good Teaching! The Case for Culturally Relevant Pedagogy." *Theory Into Practice* 34, no. 3 (1995): 160. Also see Gloria Ladson-Billings, "Toward a Theory of Culturally Relevant Pedagogy," *American Educational Research Journal* 32, no. 3 (1995): 465–91; Gloria Ladson-Billings, *The Dreamkeepers: Successful Teachers of African American Children* (San Francisco, CA: Jossey-Bass, 2009); Gloria Ladson-Billings, *Culturally Relevant Pedagogy: Asking a Different Question* (New York, NY: Teachers College Press, 2021).

20. Geneva Gay, *Culturally Responsive Teaching: Theory, Research, and Practice* (2000; reis., New York, NY: Teachers College Press, 2018), 37.

21. Django Paris, "Culturally Sustaining Pedagogy: A Needed Change in Stance, Terminology, and Practice," *Educational Researcher* 41, no. 3 (2012): 93–97. Django Paris and H. Samy Alim, "What Are We Seeking to Sustain through Culturally Sustaining Pedagogy? A Loving Critique Forward." *Harvard Educational Review* 84, no. 1 (2014): 85–100. Django Paris and H. Samy Alim, *Culturally Sustaining Pedagogies: Teaching and Leaning for Justice in a Changing World*

(New York, NY: Teachers College Press, 2017). Gloria Ladson-Billings, "Culturally Relevant Pedagogy 2.0: a.k.a. The Remix," *Harvard Educational Review* 84, no. 1 (2014): 74–84.

22. Paris and Alim, *Culturally Sustaining Pedagogies*, 3.

23. Andrew Wright, *Critical Religious Education*.

24. Wright, *Critical Religious Education*, 104.

25. Christina Easton, Angela Goodman, Andrew Wright, and Angela Wright, *Critical Religious Education in Practice: A Teacher's Guide for the Secondary Classroom* (Oxfordshire: Routledge, 2019), vii.

26. Pope Francis, "Evangelii gaudium: 'The Joy of the Gospel,'" www.vatican.va, 2013.

27. Paul Griffiths, *Religious Reading: The Place of Reading in the Practice of Religion* (New York: Oxford University Press, 1999), 8–10.

28. Angela Valenzuela, *Subtractive Schooling: U.S.-Mexican Youth and the Politics of Caring* (Albany, NY: State University of New York Press, 1990).

29. Paulo Freire, trans. Robert R. Barr, *Pedagogy of Hope: Reliving Pedagogy of the Oppressed* (1994; reis., London: Bloomsbury Academic, 2014).

30. Valerie Kinloch, "'You Ain't Making Me Write': Culturally Sustaining Pedagogies and Black Youths' Performances of Resistance," *Culturally Sustaining Pedagogies: Teaching and Leaning for Justice in a Changing World* (New York: Teachers College Press, 2017), 25–42, 29, emphasis hers.

# 12

# HOLY ENVY, INTERRELIGIOUS ENGAGEMENT AND RECONCILIATION
## One Orthodox Christian's Perspective

*Eleni Lampadarios*

Silence prevailed in the auditorium. The Upper School Community of Friends School of Baltimore had just been told that a beloved physical education teacher had died and a Meeting for Worship had been called so that we could be together and reflect upon his life. As I sat there with my advisees in the upper balcony, I was struck by the spiritual power that this silence seemed to hold. I didn't know this teacher at all, as I had been at Friends School of Baltimore for only a couple of months and our paths hadn't crossed. However, through this silence, I could feel a connection with those who had known him. The silence was broken at times by students and employees standing up to share memories of this teacher who had clearly been a positive force during his time at Friends. After I left that meeting, I told one of the Quaker faculty members in the Upper School how amazing it was to have something in place like Meeting for Worship that the school could turn to in times of need. The students didn't need any reminders on how to begin meeting. It just happened. That was more than a decade ago. Since then, as an Upper School History teacher at Friends School of Baltimore, I have experienced countless Meetings for Worship. Even though not all of them have been as spiritual as that one, I have come to depend upon this Quaker practice as a way for me to deepen my connections with my school community and to deepen my own prayer and reflective practice.

I was raised in and continue to practice a faith where silence is not a part of worship practice. My ethnic background is Greek, and Eastern Orthodoxy is a tradition that embraces what I like to call a full-body worship. Every one of the five senses is called to worship the Trinitarian God. When one enters an Orthodox church, one will immediately see icons in the front of the church shielding the altar in the iconostasis as well as behind the altar and along the sides. The services are mostly chanted or sung by the priest, *psalti* (chanters), and possibly a choir. The smell of the incense at certain points in the service helps re-engage us if our minds have wandered. Even the frequency and way in which Orthodox Christians cross themselves (three fingers pressed together touching the forehead, navel, right shoulder, and left shoulder) builds a connection between us and God. And, finally, the climax of the Divine Liturgy, Holy Communion—where we "Taste the Body of Christ" and "Drink the Cup of Immortality"—forms in us the ultimate connection that we individually and communally can have with Jesus.

From this description of Eastern Orthodoxy, one can see that it is pretty much the polar opposite of a Quaker Meeting for Worship. So, what can I gain from a religious practice that is so different from my own? For some, perhaps many, Orthodox, finding value in this Quaker practice could seem impossible. How could worship without a priest or any prescribed leader, spoken prayers, intercessions, processions, and other sacred acts be worship of any kind? Indeed, even worship in any Christian tradition outside of Orthodoxy would likely be considered a non-starter for some. For as long as I can remember, I have been someone who has felt comfortable in a non-Orthodox Christian setting even though I am completely at home in an Orthodox one. Attending a secondary school in the Episcopal tradition, participating in non-denominational Bible studies in college, and connecting with other Christians through the Taizé community, an ecumenical movement based in France, has meant that I have been a member of a Christian minority denomination in a dominant Christian culture for most of my life. The only time I wasn't in the minority was when I lived in Russia for six months during my junior year in college. Even though the people I worshiped with were also Orthodox, they gave me new practices to deepen my worship. Ultimately, I had two choices in my life when it came to developing my worship practice: I could have avoided all other forms of worship and stuck with Orthodox services and fellowship—even though those opportunities were pretty limited at times—or I could continue to seek and connect with God through any way possible. I chose the second option, and it has brought me great joy, connections, and growth in ways I couldn't have imagined. Last year, when I was a teaching fellow at the Institute for Islamic, Christian, and Jewish Studies (ICJS) in Baltimore, MD, I learned what to call this approach: "Holy Envy."

"Holy Envy" can be a powerful tool in creating a society where learning and understanding different religious experiences and beliefs is a normal and well-developed practice. Krister Stendahl, a biblical scholar from Sweden, coined the term, "holy envy" in the 1980s,  in response to opposition towards the opening of a Mormon temple in Stockholm. According to Barbara Brown Taylor, Stendahl introduced "three rules of religious understanding," one of which was "Leave room for holy envy;" Taylor also admits that it wasn't fully clear what Stendahl meant.[1] My introduction to holy envy, which I understand to be the idea that we can admire and respect other religious traditions without diluting our own, was through the ICJS course, "Jesus at the Border of Judaism and Islam," by ICJS Jewish Scholar Benjamin Sax. The concept became especially relevant for me when I listened to the co-teacher of this course, ICJS Muslim Scholar Zeyneb Sayilgan, speak so lovingly about Jesus and Mary and their importance as religious figures in Islam, that I came to understand how Muslims and Christians could both love Jesus and Mary despite the differences in beliefs. Engaging in this interreligious course, reading Taylor's book, and reflecting on my own religious practices, have strengthened my awareness of how much holy envy plays in my life and how it should not be taken for granted. This in my view is especially important, considering how attractive the Orthodox Church has appeared to some white nationalists.

Learning and understanding how white supremacy and Christianity intersect, particularly how Christian language and teachings have manifested themselves in this doctrine, is an important step in building racial reconciliation. Until recently, I mostly thought of this intersection as being primarily grounded in the White Protestant tradition as evidenced by the participation and leadership of White Christians in the January 6, 2021 insurrection at the U.S. Capitol. The Fellowship lecture by ICJS Protestant Scholar Matthew D. Taylor on "White Supremacy, Christian Nationalism, and What Does It Have to Do with Jews and Muslims?" given soon after this event brought to light that antisemitism and Islamophobia have deep roots in the Christian tradition and once-mainstream Christian ideas. Yet, Taylor also noted, "Many Christians are ignorant of or naively detached from those elements of Christian history and theology." For too long, I have fallen into this camp of Christians. Even though I am very much aware of the ethnocentric and nationalistic strain that can be part of the Orthodox Church, I have seen my identity as a member of a minority Christian group whose early history in the U.S. was filled with their own experiences of discrimination as being outside of the reaches of White Supremacy. The history of the Orthodox Church in America was primarily an immigrant story, and a relatively recent one. Indeed, some early Greek immigrants were victims of the Ku Klux Klan; so there's a history of being discriminated against by White Protestants. But, as I was reading the news and social media posts following the events of January 6, 2021, it became clear to me that I had to come to terms with the reality that the Orthodox Church in the U.S. has its own problem with White Supremacy as there was clear evidence that Orthodox Christians participated in the attack, including a priest who was suspended for his participation.

Although my work in understanding the infiltration of white supremacists in Orthodoxy is just beginning, others in the Church have been sounding the alarms for a while. Katie Kelaidis, who studies Medieval Christianity and contemporary Orthodox identity, has written several articles in the online journal, *Religion Dispatches*, concerning the presence of white supremacists in the Orthodox Church. In her article from November 30th, 2016, entitled, "How Orthodox Christianity Became the Spiritual Home of White Nationalism," Dr. Kelaidis explains why the Orthodox Church has attracted white supremacists. She states white nationalists use the Byzantine and Russian empires as examples of states that stood their ground. Even though these empires eventually fell, the story that is told points to enemy forces—the Ottomans and the Soviets—being at fault. She writes: "In short, it is easy to tell the story of Orthodox empires in a way that conforms ever so perfectly to the view of history that propels white nationalism. And conversion to Orthodoxy offers the wanna-be Christian soldier a real-life medieval institution, battered by Muslims and Marxists, in which to make his stand."[2] For many of these converts, President Vladimir Putin is heralded as an anti-democratic leader because they "see themselves as oppressed by democracy because democracy is really diversity."[3] According to the Alexei Krindatch, a sociologist of religion, who was interviewed for an NPR article in May 2022, there has been a growth in the number of parishes in the ROCOR (Russian Orthodox Church Abroad) in the past decade, and that many of these parishes were founded by converts to Orthodoxy.[4] I worry about how the attractiveness of Orthodoxy to some White Supremacists could impact the possibilities for holy envy, for these encounters wouldn't reveal what I consider to be the true nature of the Orthodox Church. It also impedes the efforts of the Church to engage in the necessary work of racial reconciliation

Even though, until recently, I didn't know how to label what I was doing when I engaged with non-Orthodox Christians, this was something that has always felt mostly natural and comfortable to me, especially compared to the racial reconciliation work that I'm being led to engage in more prominently in the past year. It will likely take years to reconcile the events of 2020–21, particularly the deaths of Black people at the hands of police, the attacks on Asian Americans, and the violence and political drama that unfolded. It has challenged me, as an Orthodox Christian, to face the harsh injustices that Christians have perpetrated against religious and racial minorities alike, and to begin a journey on which I hope to identify and take actions within my Church and society that lead to healing. After the killings of Breonna Taylor and George Floyd, and the protests that followed last spring, the leadership of the Greek Orthodox Archdiocese hosted a series of conversations with Orthodox Christians on topics pertaining to racial reconciliation. Through these conversations, I have been introduced to Black Americans who have converted to Eastern Orthodoxy, including the founders of the Fellowship of St. Moses the Black, which seeks to equip Orthodox Christians to engage in racial reconciliation. As I listen to members of this brotherhood share their reflections and experiences as African Americans, I find myself engaging in a different kind of holy envy. I am learning deeply about my Orthodox faith through Orthodox Christians whose culture, history, and experiences are different from mine; it is many of these individuals who are leading the work of racial reconciliation within the Church.

Holy envy continues to enrich my spiritual life. It has put me in the crossroads of religious traditions beyond and within Orthodoxy. Holy envy inspires me to live as an Orthodox Christian to the best of my ability; and, as a teacher in a fairly diverse Quaker school, I feel doubly called to be open to the possibilities of holy envy as a recipient and possibly a source. I have shared my religious background, practices, and beliefs with the students in the Community and Solitude course, which serves as the religious studies course at Friends School of Baltimore. These conversations have sometimes served as practice for students to have additional religious discussions with practitioners of faiths beyond the school community. At first, I was nervous discussing such personal and important beliefs and practices to students, some of whom I knew, some I didn't. However, I came to see these times as opportunities for holy envy encounters. Whether or not the students were religious didn't matter, I think; they could listen to how I lived my faith and take whatever they wanted to from the conversations. Having these conversations have helped me feel more comfortable sharing my religious views and practices with students in a casual setting. While Quakerism is the foundation which binds and guides the community of Friends School of Baltimore, my Orthodox Christian faith is welcome to be a part of it. By respecting and celebrating individual truths, we aim to strengthen our community.

## For Reflection:

1   Are there limits to "holy envy" in a school setting?

2   How can a religious community respond to white nationalism?

3   How can members of a school community converse comfortably about religious beliefs and practices?

# NOTES

1. Barbara Brown Taylor, *Holy Envy: Finding God in the Faith of Others* (New York: Harper, 2019), 64–66.

2. Katherine Kelaidis, "How Orthodox Christianity Became the Spiritual Home of White Nationalism," November 30, 2016, religiondispatches.org.

3. Odette Yousef, "Orthodox Christian churches are drawing in far-right American converts," npr.com, May 10, 2022.

4. Odette Yousef.

# 13

# CONFESSIONS OF A RELIGIOUS "NONE" EDUCATOR
## A Call for Dialogue and Engagement

*Travis Henschen*

I think it's been a wonderful experience, Quakerism. It's been great to learn about it and it's the religion I most identify with, I think. Because it's the religion that's never up-in-your-face. Not because the school doesn't do that at all, but because Quakerism's value system implies simplicity and isn't forced upon me. It implies pacifism. So, it aligns well with my personal beliefs and it's easy for me to assimilate to this kind of environment.

This is how I concluded my conversation with a 10th-grade student who has attended our Quaker school since kindergarten about his experience of religion at school. I spoke with him after having reflected upon a series of conversations and other learning in which I engaged with a cohort of teachers from the Baltimore area about teaching religion. He had just presented in front of a group of prospective students and their caregivers on an admissions panel and his remarks about the role of religion in our school were timely and relevant. At the time, I was reflecting on the rise of religious "nones" among the high-school aged population. His concluding remarks aligned well with my impression of many of my students' views on the "issue" of religious disaffiliation: while our young people are less likely to identify with a particular religion or religion at all, they are open to engaging in dialogue about religion—especially as it relates to their conception of spirituality and connection to social issues they care about.

I am an administrator and history teacher at the Friends School of Baltimore, a 236-year-old Quaker school. The school's religious identity is clearly articulated in its mission statement: "Recognizing that there is that of God in each person, the School strives in all its programs, policies, and affairs to be an institution that exemplifies the ideals of the Religious Society of Friends." In addition to Friends School's commitment to the Quaker values of simplicity, peace, integrity, community, equality, and stewardship, students and staff regularly gather for what Quakers call Meeting for Worship. Our youngest learners in elementary and middle school engage in more deliberate Meetings and emphasis is placed on Quaker values within the classroom. While students are not required to take Quakerism or religion courses, faculty do not shy away from incorporating religion in their core and elective course offerings.

When we were physically together before school shutdowns due to the COVID-19 pandemic, we gathered for Meetings about once a week in a variety of spaces: the auditorium, the Stony Run Meetinghouse adjacent to our school buildings, and even in classrooms and outdoor spaces across campus. Meeting for Worship's rituals flow directly out of the Quaker belief that there is "that of God" in every person. There are no sacraments or clergy because Quakers believe that worship consists of personal communion with God. We enter the space quietly and settle ourselves in auditorium seats, on simple wooden benches, in classroom chairs, or on the grass. Sometimes, we begin with a query for reflection. Then comes silence. Participants may stand to speak, if they feel so moved.

Before Friends, I taught at a Jesuit Catholic high school and an all-girls Catholic high school in Baltimore. At the Jesuit school, most of our students were not Catholic. The entire school gathered for Mass a few times a year. Like my students, I knew what it felt like to attend a Catholic Mass without a deep, personal connection to the rituals and practices. As a gay Millennial from a majority-Protestant family who chose public school over private or religious schools, I was already uncomfortable with the Catholic Church's stance on homosexuality, gender expression, and the role of women within the Church's power structure. I attended Mass with our majority non-Catholic students and majority-Catholic faculty, using the time to reflect and feel connected with members of our school community.

Almost a decade of employment at religious schools has led my closest friends and family members to ask, "Why do you, of all people, like working in those places?" Confession: I love teaching religion, discussing religion, and working in religious schools. But I'm a religious "none." And so are many—perhaps most—of my students. According to the Pew Research Center, a religious "none" is a person who does not identify or affiliate with a religion. They can be atheists, agnostics, or "nothing in particular." Religiously unaffiliated people have been growing as a share of all

Americans for several decades. Not surprisingly, religious "nones" are concentrated among young adults more than any other age group. At least 35 percent of Millennials are religiously unaffiliated.[1]

Occasionally, our ICJS Teachers Fellowship cohort discussed the fact that young people today seem to be increasingly unaffiliated with organized religion. "The problem with society today is that we've moved away from religion," one cohort member argued. He commented on the apparent lack of empathy and moral fortitude in some of his students and viewed the rise in religious "nones" to be a problem to be solved.

I asked our student the extent to which he believes adults should be concerned about the rise of religiously unaffiliated youth. He replied:

> I really don't think they should be concerned about how religious we are. That whole idea of people should be religious is something that has been prominent throughout history and is forcing them to think that way about us. I also think older generations tend not to readily accept new ways of thinking. For example, seniors often "do not like" underclassmen in school. The youth not being as religious—I really don't believe that. I think in some cases that may be true but that's because more people are identifying with scientific ways of thinking.

As one of the cohort's younger teachers and one of the only religious nones, I became frustrated with the line of discussion and thinking that characterized these shifts in religious identity among youth as a problem. If it really is a problem, then I'm part of the problem. How intentionally and effectively do our schools create spaces for authentic, interreligious dialogue and exploration? What role and obligations do educators have in creating these spaces and learning opportunities?

Nothing in my upbringing or decade of teaching experience made me believe that young people are not interested in religion. Nor does it appear that they have rejected it as an important institution or aspect of identity. As an adolescent, I remember lively debates and discussions about religion in history and English classes, and around campfires with my closest friends. As a leader in my Scout troop as a high schooler, I often co-led our troop in prayer—despite my status as a religious none. At one point, I was even asked to deliver a homily. In college—a secular institution, I might add—my peers engaged in interfaith programming and signed up for extra religion courses to better understand the rapidly changing world. In my freshman year, all students had to grapple with a common set of texts in a "core" course, many of which explored religion; professor- and student-led discussions guided us to make connections between the texts and our own identity development and emerging worldview.

At the majority non-Catholic Catholic school in downtown Baltimore where I taught, I attended weekend "Kairos" retreats, a hallmark of Jesuit schools. Our students bonded with each other in ways I never witnessed in the classroom or during Mass. They sometimes challenged the religious beliefs of both their families and the school, while at the same time exploring their spirituality and religious identity that sometimes just didn't fit within the framework provided by the adults. Their questions were similar to the ones I contemplated as an adolescent, many of which I still haven't been able to answer as an adult.

At Friends, another one of my former students identifies as Buddhist (a departure from his family's religious tradition) and is teaching himself Sanskrit to be able to engage with important texts directly. As I mentioned before, all students, no matter their religious identity, gather for shared worship each week. Some choose to stand and speak, sharing both personal struggles and joys, and many times reflecting on their spirituality and experience of religion. I wonder if youth today are equally as curious about religion as they were in previous generations—perhaps even more so.

I asked one boy how Quakerism at Friends aligns with his family's traditions and history. He shared:

> I grew up in a Christian family, but I never identified with Christianity. My mother and father were Christian, and my mom was more strict about it than my dad. They never forced us to go to church or anything like that. I grew up with more of a connection to scientific ways of thinking as opposed to religious ways of thinking. I shared with the admissions panel that Quakerism is present in the school, but you see more of the values of Quakerism than the religious part of it. I can focus more on the values and ignore the religious aspects. I was talking about Meeting for Worship. I appreciate that, during Meeting for Worship, it's not just one person running it and telling you what to believe; rather, it's more of a communal group. One can have one's own beliefs, but not be dominated by someone else with different beliefs. You can be yourself in that space.

He went on to share about his family's connection to Quakerism: "My family loves Quakerism. In our heritage, we have some connections to Quakerism and I believe it's my grandfather on my mother's side who grew up in India...they went to a Quaker school there."

Several Quakers have explored the themes illuminated in this student's responses and the "issue" of religious nones. Thomas H. Jeavons, a Quaker scholar, has reflected on the rise of religious nones as it relates to the growth and development of Quakerism. He holds that "there is a rising interest in genuine spiritual experience, as opposed to religions that focus primarily on belief as intellectual assent to a creed, or megachurches that offer dozens of programs to improve one's life but lack an intimate, experiential spiritual center."[2] In this way, Quakerism can be adapted to the current moment and provide new pathways—even for youth who are religiously unaffiliated.

As a teacher at a Quaker school, I see tremendous value in teaching students about religion—both through the formal curriculum and through co-curricular activities—because it exposes them to a more diverse range of human experience and can expand their moral and religious development to the extent they choose to affiliate with an organized religion. Students in our Quaker Student Union and Jewish Student Union, for example, teach the community about core aspects of their respective religions and engage in programming (retreats, celebrations, etc.) designed to deepen their own faith and practice and promote interreligious literacy and tolerance across the school community. On field trips and through elective courses, all students visit places of worship throughout Baltimore and engage in community service partnerships with many religiously affiliated non-profit organizations (for example, the association between the Jewish Federation of Baltimore and Catholic Charities of Baltimore). In the same way, we make space for those religious groups and provide opportunities for interreligious engagement for students, schools should embrace religious nones and provide space for them to openly discuss their experiences of religion.

But the "problem" of religious disaffiliation identified in my ICJS Teachers Fellowship cohort extends beyond younger populations. Ryan Burge, a political scientist who has studied the rise of religious nones, reminds us that the rise of religious disaffiliation is not limited to the youth demographic. He holds that there is evidence that older members of our society are abandoning their faith communities later in life.[3] In light of Burge's findings, the concerns of my cohort members and colleagues about our students' religious affiliation seem misplaced. How might we as educators develop core interreligious dialogue practices in our intergenerational school communities so that we can better understand each other's histories, identities, and shared values? To me, this is a more useful question and issue to raise as we explore religion with young people.

I recently teamed up with our school's newly-appointed Director of Quaker Life and an English teacher who also participated in the ICJS Teachers Fellowship to re-launch our Quaker Student Union that had become inactive during the COVID years. Not knowing what to expect, we put out an open call to the upper school student body to gauge interest in re-activating the group, starting with a retreat to Pendle Hill, a Quaker retreat center just outside Philadelphia. We were pleased to discover that a diverse range of students expressed interest in attending. In the initial information session, many students asked if they needed to be Quaker to attend the retreat. We explained that only a very small percentage of our student body and faculty identify as Quaker, and that all were welcome to attend. Even though we had not set out to engage in interreligious dialogue during the information session, the questions students asked pointed to their curiosity about religion and, for many, their developing sense of spirituality and even faith. Some students shared their religious affiliation while others openly shared that they were not religious. It seems that even the mere invitation to a Quaker retreat created space for young people and adults of a range of faith backgrounds, including religious nones, to come together to explore and improve Quakerism and religious life at school.

As we walk alongside our students on their journey to form their identities and a sense of purpose, is it our business to decide whether they are religious enough? Have we given young people enough room and support to develop their religious identities? The rise in religious nones is occurring across age groups, not just Millennials and Gen Z. Based on my year-long experience in the ICJS cohort, I want to engage more intentionally in dialogue with my students about their experience of religion and expose them to the incredible religious diversity of the United States and the world.

## FOR REFLECTION

1   How can educators in secular or faith-based schools create spaces for engagement in interreligious dialogue and that intentionally include the voices of people who are not affiliated religiously?

2   To what extent do the reflections shared by the Quaker school student quoted in this essay resonate with your experience?

3   How can external demands for improvement of religious literacy be balanced with some students' interest in further faith formation?

# NOTES

1. Michael Lipka, "A closer look at America's rapidly growing religious 'nones'," Pew Research Center (May 13, 2015).

2. Thomas H. Jeavons, "Sharing Our Faith with The Nones," *Friends Journal* (December 1, 2013).

3. Ryan P. Burge, *The Nones: Where They Came From, Who They Are, And Where They Are Going* (Minneapolis, MN: Fortress Press, 2021), 93.

Part IV

# Outside and Beyond
# Secondary Education

# 14

# THE LUMINOUS CROSSROADS OF FAITH AND CIVIC LEARNING
## Meeting the Challenge of Navigating Diversity

*Lindsay Bressman*

The challenge of navigating diversity without devolving into harmful polarization is as old as history; likewise, the quest to establish societies in which difference is not only tolerated but also embraced as an asset and strength. The birth of self-governance promoted the notion that liberty would not be limited to a particular lineage, but could be experienced and obtained by all. Appallingly, this pursuit of freedom omitted swaths of people—from indigenous residents whose land had been conquered to Africans forced into slavery. Distinct, at times cruel, barriers to independence and freedom were erected along race, culture, origin, ethnicity, class, religion, and gender lines. While surely not being practiced fully, the groundwork for imagining a pluralist America was delineated within the First Amendment's opening clause, "Congress shall make no law respecting an establishment of religion, or prohibiting the free exercise thereof." That eighteenth-century declaration was a far cry from the ways in which religion had been historically, and continues to be, a source of conflict and warfare. Our pursuit of true religious freedom and pluralism remains a North Star, while differences are fierce and antagonistic, and divisions grow more destructive each day. With a demographic mosaic as vibrant as the ocean floor, is it possible to create an actual pluralistic peoplehood? How do we make inter-group connections of mutual respect accessible and realistic? With an eye to the future, can we plant seeds of compassion, love, friendship, and resourcefulness in the next generation? What types of learning should educators provide students so that they are empowered to navigate an ever-evolving, complex American society? Civic Spirit is an initiative that offers an answer to these questions.

Civic Spirit has demonstrated that faith-inspired, multi-modal civics education can be a vital pedagogy for fostering civic responsibility in secondary school students toward a productive, healthy, and peaceful society. Civic Spirit's programs derive insight from ancient religious rites of passage, such as the Jewish *b'nai mitzvah* (child of the commandment). One origin of the *b'nai mitzvah* can be tied to a demarcation of the 13th year of life, as this was the age when the core education of Biblical characters Esau and Jacob appears to end and their paths diverge. The Talmud (the central text of Rabbinic Judaism and the primary source of Jewish religious law) includes *Baruch Sheptarani*—a prayer from Isaac, the father of Esau and Jacob: "Blessed is He who has now freed me from the responsibility of this [child]."[1] The language seems to imply that parents or the adults of a community are obligated to provide a specific body of knowledge and experience to youth in guiding their path to maturity; but, at some point, adults must relinquish their ability to dictate the choices of the next generation. In considering this model, the periods of childhood and formal schooling are acutely relevant.

Civic Spirit recognizes that secondary school education is a precious period of learning, reflecting, practicing, and becoming participating members of society. It features, therefore, a three-pillared approach that integrates and engages the whole person—the sacred realm of mind, body, and soul. By providing educators and schools from a diverse network with high-caliber professional development based on this methodology, Civic Spirit encourages dynamic civic education that can inspire, inform, and empower students to foster appreciation and agency over their role in shaping the future. How does it work? Here are three illustrations.

## OUTCOME #1:

Faith-inspired civics education explores the complex dynamic between religion and democracy in deeply diverse America.

### STUDY OF TEXT: LINCOLN'S SECOND INAUGURAL ADDRESS

In August 2019, in the sweltering heat of New York City, two men sat side-by-side at a seminar table: a 40-year-old, third-generation rabbi from a modern orthodox school and a 70-year-old Puerto Rican deacon who teaches Spanish and Public Debate at a Catholic-inspired middle school serving under-resourced students. Together, they read aloud Abraham Lincoln's Second Inaugural Address, delivered March 4, 1865, as the Civil War was drawing to a close with the Unionists as the likely victor. Words of faith, confusion, anger, gratitude, and redemption jumped off the page:

> If we shall suppose that American slavery is one of those offenses which, in the providence of God, must needs come, but which—having continued through His appointed time—He now wills to remove, and that He gives to both North and South this terrible war, as the woe due to those by whom the offense came, shall we discern therein any departure from those divine attributes which the believers in a living God always ascribe to Him? Fondly do we hope—fervently do we pray—that this mighty scourge of war may speedily pass away. Yet, if God wills that it continue until all the wealth piled by the bondsman's two hundred and fifty years of unrequited toil shall be sunk, and until every drop of blood drawn with the lash shall be paid by another drawn with the sword, as was said three thousand years ago, so still it must be said: "the judgments of the Lord are true and righteous altogether."[2]

From the close reading of this pivotal text by the rabbi and the deacon, important questions emerged. If God saw injustice and decided to intervene with war and chose to have the war last for centuries, as long as brutal slavery lasted, would we still revere Him? Of course. In fact, a drawn-out war would be the only form of atonement worthy of humankind's horrid behavior. And yet the Civil War only lasted four years. Why? Had God extended His mercy and given us a second chance? Contrastingly, hadn't slavery transpired under God's watch? Can we believe in national redemption? In the face of one of humankind's most egregious acts, God gave us the possibility of beginning again—can we heed His call, the educators debated, and move our nation towards the ideal of equality for all?

### Civic Belonging:

At its 2020 Summer Institute, Civic Spirit hosted an interfaith text study of three pivotal prayers (Christian, Jewish, Muslim) that speak about our atonement and God's forgiveness. In small groups, educators were asked to consider how the religious traditions of atonement and forgiveness can be applied to group and individual wrongdoings within our current social order; essentially, can religious ritual strengthen American democracy? Is there a version of atonement and forgiveness that can be integrated into our nation's stories of pain and destruction?

During the same institute, educators participated in a dialogue training workshop, engaging in discussion and full-spectrum active listening on vulnerable prompts, such as: Who or what do you consider to be your community? When do you feel you belong? When do you feel you don't fit in? How do faith and religion fit into your sense of community and belonging?[3]

## Civic Skills:

In mid-October 2020, six months into a catastrophic pandemic and days before a fiercely divided presidential election, a group of students from across the U.S. joined a virtual session entitled, "Will Your Vote Match Your Values?" in partnership with the organization Vote by Design. The goal of the workshop was two-fold: to review the six functions of the President of the United States, as stated by Article 2 of the US Constitution; and to help students recognize the understandable biases they bring to a conversation about what kind of person should serve as U.S. President. In consideration of the president's responsibilities, students were asked to consider factors including previous experience, leadership qualities, and personal attributes such as whether the candidate owns a pet or is religious. This last item promoted a vibrant conversation, since many of the students attending the session were part of a faith community: Should our president be religious or of faith? If so, how religious must a president be? Does it matter what religion they are? To practice articulating their ideas and to become more aware of how those ideas had evolved, students were asked to complete the sentence, "I used to think that the president...but now I think..." One student reminded the group of the importance of this discussion and the power he and his peers hold by sharing a powerful statement attributed to Frederick Douglass: "It's easier to raise strong children than to repair broken men."

## Outcome #2:

Faith-inspired civic education uncovers where religion has endorsed injustice as well as celebrates the historic role of faith communities as critical civic agents for equality.

### Text Study: Guides for Behavior

As the Southern Christian Leadership Conference prepared to lead an action campaign against segregation in Birmingham in 1963, Martin Luther King Jr asked volunteers to sign a Commitment Card.[4] Three of the ten "commandments" on the commitment card explicitly identified God as the source of strength. King emphasized to the volunteers that they would need to rely upon their faith to resist using violence against the violent acts to which they undoubtedly would be subjected during the Birmingham protests. King and his brave partners were people of faith who understood that their love of God, and His love for them, could serve as motivation for the pursuit of justice and a tool for protection against injustice. At a Civic Spirit event for both students and parents, individuals were asked to read Martin Luther King's Commitment Card, the Ten Commandments as found in the biblical Book of Exodus, and Benjamin Franklin's "Thirteen virtues." They were then asked to consider their own commitments and what guides their behavior as participants in civic society.

## Civic Belonging:

In Fall 2021, two groups of students from demographically disparate faith-based schools came together for a semester to create a Civic Action Committee. Their goals were to discuss current civic issues, choose one civic problem to focus on, engage in research, and develop an action project to address the issue they collectively chose. As demands of school and other extracurricular obligations usurped their time, the students realized that developing an action project was unrealistic; however, they enjoyed engaging in honest discussions of civic matters and forming authentic relationships with one another, an integral connection necessary for building American pluralism.

## Civic Skills:

Every year, a group of students from the Civic Spirit network is selected to join the Delegates Program and train as civic ambassadors for their school and local community. Students have focused on a variety of topics such as youth service, the U.S. Census, the economy, and election legislation. The goal of the Delegates Program is to give students the opportunity to learn in-depth about a key civic matter and to practice the art of problem-solving.

As an example, in 2021, the students studied the history and practice of ranked choice voting (RCV), which would be introduced to New York City for the mayoral primary election. The Delegates identified that lack of understanding about this new practice could negatively impact voting participation, and so they wrote and produced a public service announcement to educate adults on how to complete a RCV ballot.

Students who complete the Delegates Program possess greater knowledge of governmental and societal systems and richer awareness of themselves and their peers. A delegate from the third cohort remarked:

> It was phenomenal, I had the chance to learn with and from such an incredibly diverse group—both educators and students alike. At first, I thought that it would be hard for us to communicate and understand each other, especially since I've led a pretty cloistered life and mostly just associated myself with my community.

However, after exchanging ideas and thoughts, I realized that we were so similar and cared about many of the same causes. We all wanted to create safe platforms for people in our schools, for people we felt were underrepresented. With patience, curiosity, and the help of our mentors, We were able to create a project we felt would resonate with our school community at large.

## Outcome #3:

Faith-inspired civics education promotes religious literacy and authentic inter-group relationships across religious, racial, cultural, and socio-economic differences.

## Text Study: The Bible on Consus-Taking

On November 14, 2019, educators working with Civic Spirit joined a nonpartisan interfaith Day of Learning on "The U.S. Census: Historic, Civic, Ethical & Religious Considerations: What Counts, Who Counts, and Who Decides?" In small groups, the teachers engaged in analytic reading of the 1900, 1950, and 2000 U.S. Census forms and archived and current data maps.[5] They looked at how questions have changed over time, what data points, such as race, gender, ethnicity, gender identity, and citizen status, have been gathered over the years, and what historical trends and factors have impacted these decisions. To ground the relevance of the census in religious traditions of counting, three educators were invited to teach passages from the Bible that reference census-taking: Luke 2:1–2 and Numbers 1 and 26.

### Civic Belonging:

In Spring 2019, mindful of the swirling existential unrest our nation was feeling, Civic Spirit launched a campaign in partnership with art luminary For Freedoms to elevate the power of prayer. Educational materials were curated for teachers at Civic Spirit-affiliated schools to infuse their curriculum with a study of the function of prayer as a form of gratitude, praise, request, or wish. Resources included six different prayers for our country chanted in a variety of religious services. The Prayer for America project challenged students across the Civic Spirit network to create their own prayer using the prompts: "What are you grateful for? What do you hope for in a government designed by and for the people?" Over 50 students submitted awe-inspiring messages revealing their concerns, dreams, and commitments. Two students from different religions were selected to chant their prayers publicly at Civic Spirit Day, an all-day convening for students to design solutions to civic issues.

One of the students' prayers opened with, "For our community, I pray that the walls which separate us will not hold us back. I pray that we will not allow division of thought and belief to confine us. I pray that instead of simply sustaining the walls which divide us, we can build bridges between them." A digital mosaic was created of the prayers and photos of the students, which was then distributed as a poster for all participating Civic Spirit schools.

### Civic Skills:

In the summer of 2020, a group of Muslim, Jewish, and Catholic teens met on Zoom for a virtual cafe hour. Trapped at home in the middle of the pandemic, they were eager for connection and hungry for purpose. In the first session, each student was invited to practice empathetic listening and thoughtful storytelling by addressing the prompt, "Please share with us a moment in your life that helps to explain your American story." The differences among the students were profound; as a result, there were both tears and warm, compassionate smiles. Students were also invited to ask one another questions about their religious practice. They inquired about clothing, food, observance, and religious text. There was no judgment—just curiosity and listening. The students chose to meet again, and again, identifying causes they are passionate about and exploring what in their faith traditions inspires their desire for civic participation. This ad hoc group culminated in an in-person event in Spring 2021 in which the students created care packages of sustainability products, such as reusable cutlery, to send to members of their respective communities.

## CONCLUSION:

If religious pluralism is the goal, our children present an opportunity to achieve a world in which that state of being can be real. How might we equip students to do so? Engage their hearts, heads, and hands. In preparing the next generation for inheriting the consequential responsibility of preserving democracy, Civic Spirit believes that youth can be best supported in embodying this role by engaging them at varied access points—from the physical to the ephemeral—including text study, civic belonging, and essential skills for communication and problem-solving. With appreciation for the centrality of educators, Civic Spirit also prioritizes teachers' learning by providing them with intellectually, emotionally, and spiritually fulfilling enrichment—as they are truly on the front lines of our nation's future.

## FOR REFLECTION

1   What role do you think religion plays in democracy? Does the practice of religion strengthen or harm democratic ideas?

2   What religious rituals can inform social dynamics in multi-faith and secular America?

3   To what extent, if at all, does it feel appropriate to study religious texts and liturgy in the context of youth education and civic learning?

# NOTES

1. Midrash Lekach Tov, Genesis 25:27:1.

2. Transcribed, with adjustments to punctuation, from the fair copy manuscript of Abraham Lincoln, *Second Inaugural Address* (March 4, 1865) held by the Library of Congress.

3. M. Herzig and L. Chasin, *Fostering Dialogue Across Divides: A Nuts and Bold Guide* (Cambridge, MA: Essential Partners, 2019).

4. Stephanie Van Hook, "Why Martin Luther King's pledge of nonviolence matters today," in *Waging Nonviolence: People Powered News and Analysis* (January 18, 2016).

5. United States Census Bureau. "History and Questionnaires: Through the Decades." https://www.census.gov.

# 15
# INTERFAITH EXPERIENTIAL EDUCATION
## Identity, Perspective, Action

*Megan Hopkins*

Why do your chicken fingers look different than mine?

*Oh, that's because I eat kosher.*

What does that mean?

*Well, let me explain!*

This conversation could easily be heard amid a buzzing summer camp dining hall at lunchtime, in between plans being made for basketball games, canoe races, and discussions of the best friendship bracelet-making techniques. And on the way back to the cabin, new friends will remind each other to pray before taking their afternoon rest. It would be a common sight to see those who are not Muslim respectfully observing their Muslim friends perform *salat* before they all play cards together in the bunk.

While the city of Boston grows in diversity, it remains educationally and spiritually segregated—split off into distinct neighborhoods and enclaves by race, ethnicity, nationality, socioeconomic class, and faith tradition.[1] The work of *Mosaic: Interfaith Youth Action* invites young people to break this pattern through intentionally engaging across differences, building interfaith communities through experiential education offered in programs ranging from three-hour long workshops to an intensive summer camp.[2]

This chapter outlines the pedagogy of interfaith experiential education, detailing three of its fruits: identity formation, perspectival awareness, and social action. By bringing David Kolb's theory of experiential education to a distinctly interfaith setting, *Mosaic* leverages common experiences as the material for intentional and reflective conversations, where youth develop their personal identities in community with one another. They are challenged and shaped by their peers to interrogate their own faith commitments, and it is through the lens of faith that youth investigate their intersectional identities in conversation with one another.[3] Youth grow in perspectival awareness, developing attentiveness to their own positionality and a capacity to interrogate situations from the perspectives of others more fully. Finally, participants apply the skills they have learned in their own communities, creating more just, equitable, and peaceful neighborhoods for themselves and their peers.

## INTERFAITH EXPERIENTIAL EDUCATION

Explicitly interfaith learning for youth ages 12–18 is still a relatively new modality, with little consensus regarding the appropriate theoretical framework to employ.[4] As a non-profit operating outside of the traditional school system, *Mosaic* works with houses of worship, schools (primarily private or charter), and other non-profit organizations to deliver programming to youth that supplements the religious education they are receiving in their home tradition(s). Partners consistently articulate a need to connect youth's desire to act for social change with their self-articulated faith identities. Here, *Mosaic* programming responds, oriented towards three long-term outcomes: *Mosaic* youth identify as members of a diverse and interfaith community; *Mosaic* youth bridge divides in their communities and beyond; *Mosaic* youth identify and act as social action changemakers.

*Mosaic*'s approach to education is experiential, aiming to provide a "holistic integrative perspective on learning that combines experience, perception, cognition, and behavior."[5] This pedagogical approach recognizes that *all* of life— the experience of living itself—teaches us. As educators, we craft particular and intentional experiential moments to leverage reflection on the broader worldviews and perspectives that our participants bring with them, and to transfer this new knowledge back to their own contexts. This approach is built on the work of David Kolb, adapting the experiential learning cycle to the interfaith space.[6] We believe youth learn most effectively through doing, engaging in action and dialogue (while having a lot of fun). In order to prepare youth for vulnerable and personal conversations around their religious and values-based identities, we focus on building a community of care where participants feel safe and trust one another. Content is delivered primarily through experiences, and always processed through reflective exercises.

Experiences and reflection happen within *Mosaic* program time, while new knowledge is cultivated through the transfer of this experience beyond the programs themselves. Experiences are opportunities for content delivery, though they may not always appear as such to the outside observer. Experiences might look like game-based learning, teambuilding exercises, or observation of a religious ritual. Through these experiences, youth have the opportunity to discover new knowledge for themselves. Didactic learning is intentionally limited. Leveraging common experiences for reflection creates an equitable space for interfaith learning, where all participants are intentionally invited into an inclusive space. The kinesthetic and embodied aspects of experiential learning are especially inviting to young people who may struggle with didactic learning.

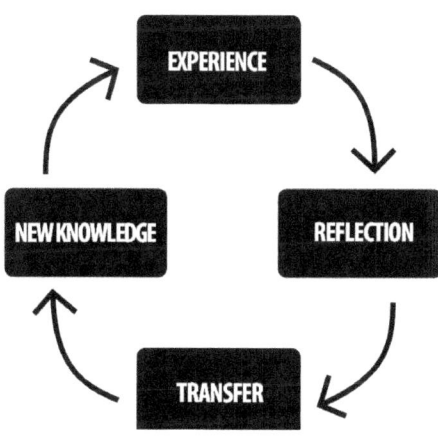

After youth share an experience together, facilitators lead them through reflections to consider what they have observed, how they have communicated with one another, how the activity made them feel.[7] This reflection time helps youth process and internalize the initial experience, allowing for a successful transfer of the experience back into their everyday lives—taking what they have learned from *Mosaic* and bringing it back to their home communities, families, schools, and faith traditions.

**Image 1: The experiential learning cycle.**
[Image created by Megan Hopkins]

Through this process, new knowledge is generated, and the cycle begins again. It is important to note that this model is a cycle, or, spiral; it does not end with a singular experience, but rather has the capacity to be deepened and shaped anew through time and circumstance.

## IDENTITY FORMATION

A common concern heard from parents when considering interfaith education regards the fear of conversion or proselytization. Any interfaith learning requires a certain amount of risk and vulnerability. It can be nerve-wracking for youth to share about their own faith identity, and it is an act of courageous vulnerability to spend time learning about other faith traditions with an open mind and humble heart.[8] Yet, it is even *more* risky for youth to be citizens of a religiously plural community and to remain ignorant of their neighbor's deeply held faith commitments.[9] To prepare young people to engage one another, *Mosaic* prioritizes community and trust-building activities at the beginning of all programs, whether they be a short three-hour program or a weeklong summer intensive. This community of care is unique each time a group assembles, comprised of the intersecting identities of all members who are present, and with an awareness and attention to those community members who may be absent. This dialogue across difference does not seek to erase difference; rather, it actively recognizes and celebrates difference, while acknowledging new points of connection and similarity.

A common activity used at *Mosaic* involves laying out a variety of objects which are central to the religious traditions of the youth who are gathered. Facilitators then allow participants to ask questions, register their curiosities or connections they might see, and pick up and investigate the objects (as appropriate). Subsequently, participants respond to each other's inquiries. Youth are invited to use "I statements" in their questions and responses, ensuring no one person is responsible for the entirety of a religious tradition, and no sweeping judgments are made. This exercise, while seemingly simple, empowers and celebrates the knowledge that participants already bring to the table, and evidences the internal diversity of each tradition. It is flexible enough to be adapted for specific seasons of the year or holidays, and adjusted to a variety of religious traditions.

These material objects serve as a catalyst for further reflection on a participant's own religious identity, visually contextualized in the broader field of religious plurality, just as the youth themselves are. While they may remain separated by religious tradition in their neighborhoods or at school, these young people are intentionally choosing to cross these invisible barriers to build bridges and reevaluate their own identities within this religiously plural context. A young person's faith identity is shaped and expanded through participation in interfaith experiential education. Participants regularly become *more* interested in their own faith tradition. As they live and learn alongside friends of other faith traditions, witnessing their prayer rituals and daily habits, playing games and having fun, participants report an increased desire to learn more deeply about their own religion, considering how they might wish to live this out in an authentic way.[10] Their self-understanding is shaped through encounter with, and through the lens of, the other.[11]

## PERSPECTIVAL AWARENESS

As participants begin to reflect on their own identity with greater depth and care, imaginative experiences invite them to next consider how the perspective of this identity shapes the ways they show up in their school, at home, and in their community. This attention to positionality can be difficult to harness for adolescents. Much of the learning done up to the point when youth come to meet us at *Mosaic* is focused on binaries.[12] Interfaith experiential education necessitates an engagement with the liminal; and, this embrace of the in-between is one that is foundational to the religious traditions of our participants. Experiential tools are uniquely suited to catalyze perspectival awareness, offering an embodied and somoaesthetic relationship with self through engagement with the other.[13]

One particular year-long *Mosaic* program brings together neighboring young people involved in their houses of worship—through youth groups or other means. This initiative works to explicitly break down the barriers of Boston's siloed neighborhoods, instead building bridges and friendships across religious divides. Youth engage in experiential activities, build skills in nonviolent communication and active listening, and spend considerable amounts of time in reflection with one another—diving deeply into dialogue across differences.

Like all activities at *Mosaic*, dialogue remains an activity that is "challenge by choice."[14] Youth sit with one another in honest, vulnerable, and open conversation. There are many ways youth can participate: through asking sincere questions, sharing their voice and opinion—or in making space for others to share theirs. It takes a significant amount of time for a group to establish their internal norms relative to dialogue, and for all participants to achieve a level of comfort in sharing their own honest perspectives. The community of care which has been established through foundational trust-building exercises is the ground on which this dialogue is able to bear fruit.

Facilitators lead participants through dialogues. Together, they consider how the issue at hand—be it climate change, systemic racism, or mental health inequities at school—impacts each person in the conversation differently, depending on their personal identities and perspective. Facilitators (be they staff or youth) rely on open-ended questions which invite participants to observe both their own emotions and reactions to the issue, and the other participants' responses. As they move through this process, groups often transition from what may be a desire for easily-won answers to grappling with the messy reality of social inequities and injustices which pervade their communities. They recognize their own positionality in these situations, not as victim or villain, but as an agent with the capacity to work for change—together with the interfaith coalition alongside them.

## Social Action

The internal impetus to work for social justice and action is strong with the youth who participate in *Mosaic* programs. One need only glance at the daily news or a social media app to discover where they find their desire. And so too, the impetus to work for social action is found internal to the myriad religious traditions *Mosaic* serves.[15] However, youth leaders and parents consistently articulate the need to connect the tenets of young people's faith traditions with this desire to improve the world around them. Youth who participate in our programs learn that bettering their communities is a central feature of living out their religious identities.

Utilizing an experiential framework, we equip youth with the skills needed to make a tangible impact in their communities. Listening intently to the young voices of our organization and the broader Boston community is foundational. *Mosaic* works closely with the Greater Boston Interfaith Organization to align our social action projects with theirs, uniting lobbying campaigns for legislative action. Oftentimes, it is through the nonpartisan legislative education offered in our program that youth learn for the first time how to make a call to their state senator or write a letter to their representative. And while our participants are too young to vote, their voice still has a tangible impact in the legislative process. This is empowering for young people, supporting their desire to continue using their voice for change into emerging adulthood and beyond.

Leadership and facilitation training is offered to our participants. These key skills extend beyond public speaking—though remaining important—to include training in group dynamics, de-escalation, and nonviolent communication. These "hard" skills pair with the "soft" skills of identity formation and perspectival awareness to equip participants to act as changemakers in their neighborhoods and communities. So too, leadership and legislative advocacy take on many forms in *Mosaic*. Art advocacy, direct action, and peer-to-peer organizing all serve different needs in the community and celebrate the unique gifts and talents of each participant. Youth recognize with startling precision the needs of their communities. And youth have the abilities to respond to these needs in their particularities: as members of religious communities, as young people, as an interfaith coalition. These intersections offer something that cannot be discounted.

## The Impact

The orientation of the experiential learning cycle is centrifugal. New knowledge is measured through its transfer beyond the primary learning environment. Reflection on experience, in dialogue, prepares participants for this movement. At *Mosaic*, participants meet one another across differences, connecting in and through new common experiences, to form interfaith friendships that transform how they see and show up in the world. Their own faith identity is clarified and their perspectival awareness is attuned. Youth are equipped to respond to recognized needs in their own communities and to leverage a groundswell of interfaith action and support for creating the peaceful, just, and equitable communities of which they dream.

## FOR REFLECTION

1 How has your own identity been challenged, clarified, or expanded through interfaith friendship and community?

2 What is an experience in your own life that has caused you to consider a situation from another person's perspective? How did you respond to this situation differently? How has this perspectival awareness changed how you show up in your own life?

3 How might the practices and pedagogical techniques elaborated in this chapter be adopted in your own learning context?

# NOTES

1. Peter Ciurczak, Antoniya Marinova, and Luc Schuster; ed., Sandy Kendall. "Kids Today: Boston's Declining Child Population and Its Effect on School Enrollment," Boston Indicators and The Boston Foundation. January 22, 2020.

2. Formerly Kids4Peace Boston. See https://mosaicaction.org/our-story/. Historically, the youth Mosaic has served have been primarily Jewish, Christian, and Muslim. The organization is in the process of making a conscious effort to expand our focus to include participants of any faith tradition.

3. See Najeeba Syeed, "Interreligious Learning and Intersectionality," in *Asian and Asian American Women in Theology and Religion,* ed. P.W. Kwok (Cham: Springer International Publishing. 2020), 171–85.

4. Debates remain regarding the appropriate age to begin interfaith learning. Concerns regarding the "ruthless confrontation" of worldviews youth experience when posed with metaphysical differences are pedagogically and theologically problematic, as expressed by Karl Nipkow. However, there have been notable shifts in the literature, where advocacy for interreligious and inter-worldview learning among youth is supported by cognitive development and educational theory. See, for instance, Carl Sterkens, *Interreligious Learning: the Problem of Interreligious Dialogue in Primary Education* (Leiden: Brill, 2001); Mohammed Abu-Nimer and R. K. Smith, "Interreligious and intercultural education for dialogue, peace and social cohesion," *International Review of Education* 62, (2016): 393–405; Didier Pollefeyt, *Interreligious Learning* (Leuven; Leuven University Press, 2007), xii., citing K.E. Nipkow, Ziele interreligiösen Lernens als Mehrdimensionales Problem, in J.A. van der Ven and H. G. Ziebertz, *Religiöser Pluralismus und Interreligiöses Lernen* (Kampen, J.H. Kok Publishing House, 1994), 197–232 at 224; Victoria Michela Garlock,"Interfaith Education for Kids," and Duncan Wielzen and Ina Ter Avest, "In Retrospect—Children's Voices on Interreligious Education," in *Interfaith Education for All: Theoretical Perspectives and Best Practices for Transformative Action*, ed. Duncan Wielzen and Ina Ter Avest (Rotterdam: Sense, 2017).

5. David A. Kolb. *Experiential Learning: Experience as the Source of Learning and Development*. Second edition. (Upper Saddle River, New Jersey: Pearson Education, 2014), 31.

6. Kolb, *Experiential Learning*, 50–64.

7. We employ a modified form of "nonviolent communication" when doing reflection. See Marshall B. Rosenberg, *Nonviolent Communication: a Language of Compassion* (Encinitas, CA: PuddleDancer Press, 1999).

8. See Marianne Moyaert, *Fragile Identities: Towards a Theology of Interreligious Hospitality* (Amsterdam: Rodopi, 2011), 277–314.

9. Diane L. Moore, "Overcoming Religious Illiteracy: Expanding the Boundaries of Religious Education." *Religious Education* 109, no. 4 (2014): 379–89.

10. Developed over time, we might recognize this as an instance of "holy envy," initially introduced by Krister Stendahl in 1985. See Hans Gustafson, *Learning from Other Religious Traditions: Leaving Room for Holy Envy* (Cham, Switzerland: Palgrave Macmillan, 2018).

11. See Catherine Cornille, *Meaning and Method in Comparative Theology* (Hoboken: Wiley, 2020), 81–93.

12. Rolf E. Muuss, *Theories of Adolescence*. Sixth Edition. (New York: McGraw Hill, 2016), 175–205.

13. See Mara Brecht, "Embodied Transactions," in *The Enigma of Divine Revelation Between Phenomenology and Comparative Theology*, ed. Jean-Luc Marion and Christiaan Jacobs-Vandegeer (Cham: Springer, 2020), 151–75.

14. "Challenge by choice" is a common principle used in ropes courses, and has been applied to adventure-based and experiential education. See Daniel L. Chase, "Does Challenge by Choice Increase Participation?" *The Journal of Experiential Education* 38, no. 2 (2015): 108–28.

15. It must be acknowledged that the particular moods and motivations to work for social action is unique to each religious tradition, and an understanding of what "justice" or "peace" may entail is as diverse internally to religious traditions as it is across religious traditions. When working with middle and high school-aged youth, finding both the similarities which connect individual participants—the impetus to work for social change—and acknowledging the different motivations for these goals is imperative for having a nuanced conversation, without moving beyond what is cognitively appropriate. See, for instance, Michael D. Palmer and Stanley M. Burgess, *The Wiley-Blackwell Companion to Religion and Social Justice* (Chichester, West Sussex: Wiley-Blackwell, 2012).

# 16
# LEARNING BEYOND SCHOOL WALLS
## Baltimore, Israel, and The Elijah Cummings Youth Program

*Kathleen St. Villier Hill*

Congressman Elijah Cummings died in 2019. I think of him daily. I am honored to manage his namesake program: The Elijah Cummings Youth Program in Israel (ECYP). Our mission:

> To invest in promising teens from Maryland's Seventh Congressional District and prepare them to serve as open-minded leaders with the skills, community ties, and global exposure critical to success in a diverse society. Our efforts are infused with the spirit of bridge-building exemplified by the longstanding relationship between the late Congressman Elijah E. Cummings and the Baltimore Jewish community.

ECYP is a space for young people to tap into their identity, learn about leadership, build community, and travel to Israel. For many of our participants, this is their first time traveling on a plane. Congressman Cummings saw the importance of providing a space outside of school time for young people in his district to explore who they are, understand their roots, and connect with the global community.

Congressman Cummings was a national figure, well-known for his leadership and advocacy in the Baltimore area and beyond. His passion for storytelling and connecting with people was evident throughout his career. He believed in the power of public speaking and used storytelling and narratives from his personal life to engage with audiences and convey the importance of various issues. A key focus of his work was on bridge-building and fostering relationships within the community. He deeply valued diversity and understood the significance of bringing people together from different backgrounds and cultures. For Congressman Cummings, this work was not just about serving his district but also about creating opportunities for young people. He was dedicated to providing educational experiences, like ECYP, which enabled students to travel and explore new places, opening doors for them and expanding their horizons. His own life was affected by such a moment of bridge-building; he often told the story of his friendship with a Jewish pharmacist who advocated for him to attend Howard University, a crucial decision that impacted the trajectory of his life. He aimed to leave a lasting legacy of empowerment and progress in his community and beyond.

We know that education is not limited to our school walls. There are spaces that can really engage young people beyond the formal classroom. ECYP has thrived as an out-of-school-time program. Many such programs operate as non-formal learning spaces. According to the Council of Europe, non-formal education is described as "outside formal learning environments but within some kind of organizational framework. It arises from the learner's conscious decision to master a particular activity, skill, or area of knowledge and is thus the result of intentional effort."[1] The learner is at the heart of a non-formal experience and remains the driver of their learning. Students demonstrate their desire to be part of a non-formal learning setting through applying for a program. By showing interest in ECYP, participants demonstrate a desire to be in a unique space to learn about leadership skills that will have an impact on their future. Congressman Cummings saw the importance of non-formal education as a space to bring together communities that could learn about their similarities and their differences. He believed in an education that is not just rooted in our school spaces because he knew of the power within his community.

ECYP has always understood the power of learning beyond a classroom. The program began in 1998 as a cultural immersion trip to Israel. It was modeled after The Leland Kibbutz Program in Israel. Mickey Leland was a U.S. Congressman from Texas who took students to Israel from his district. Congressman Cummings was approached by leaders in Baltimore's Jewish community to consider a similar program model. The program started as an opportunity to expose students in Maryland's Seventh District to Israel and the Jewish faith. In 2002, ECYP was able to expand with a gift from the late Jerold Hoffberger. The gift allowed the program to grow into a two-year fellowship that supports leadership training, community service, and a month-long trip to Israel, all of which created a richer and deeper program for students. We are supported by The Baltimore Jewish Council (BJC), an agency of The Associated: Jewish Federation of Baltimore.

The application process for the program starts in tenth grade. Students who live or go to school in Maryland's Seventh District are eligible to apply, regardless of whether they attend public, private, charter, or homeschool. The application is rigorous and includes questions about issues close to the Congressman's heart, two letters of recommendation, and transcripts. A selection committee reviews all applications and selects about twenty students for in-person interviews. Congressman Cummings often participated in these interviews, getting to know the young people in his district and what they cared about. From these interviews, twelve or thirteen students are chosen to participate in the program, aiming for a diverse group reflective of the district. The program components consist of leadership training, a cultural immersion trip to Israel in between their junior and senior years, and, during the second year, community service particularly focusing on social justice issues.

The program starts with a curriculum that explores self-identity, leadership, and relationships, focusing on building bridges between different communities. The curriculum includes workshops, field trips, and meetings with leaders at the local, state, and federal levels. In their senior year, students engage in a social justice project, working with Jewish teens to explore social justice issues and produce a podcast about their findings. The program also includes a cultural immersion trip to Israel, where students spend three and a half weeks traveling throughout the country and building relationships with Israeli peers. Upon returning, students share their experiences through storytelling and public speaking.

The ECYP process of leadership development asks young people—first, and most importantly—to learn who they are. Identity work, in my opinion, is central to leadership development. Students participate in workshops where they have an opportunity to be in extended conversations around their own selves. Through that self-discovery, they then are able to learn and be in community with someone different from themselves. In particular, ECYP explores the relationships and histories between the African-American community and the primarily white, Jewish community in Baltimore. Baltimore has a unique history of the two communities living side-by-side but often divided. We invite our students to intentionally think of Baltimore as a learning space and visit the Reservoir Hill neighborhood in which the youth explore the stories of the Jewish community and Black community in this space.[2] There are parallel and divergent histories of discrimination in Baltimore's Jewish and African-American populations, and we use this neighborhood to tell those stories.

Fifty-two percent of Maryland's Seventh Congressional District identifies as Black or African-American, according to 2020 census data. A majority of ECYP's participants are African-American with a diversity of lived experiences. This echoes participants' interactions with the diversity of Jewish communities. In Baltimore, ECYP participants meet and partner with a Jewish population that is both white and Black. In Israel, they meet with diverse teens, including Ethiopian Jewish youth and refugees. We want to be particularly thoughtful about these identities, and this mirrors Congressman Cummings's fundamental call for relationship building. These young people are bridge-builders across identities that are similar to their own and experiences that are totally different from theirs.

Savoy Adam, ECYP class of 2019, lives by the motto that "The dream is free, but the hustle is sold separately." Savoy is a hustler. He has a passion to make change and be inspired by everyone and everything that crosses his path. Savoy reminds me a lot of Congressman Cummings. Both men grew up in Baltimore City. His spirit is strong, and his voice is loud, just like Congressman Cummings'. Savoy can walk into a room and command attention, just like Congressman Cummings did.

ECYP was designed for a student like Savoy. He saw that his high school had a strong Black and Jewish population but often spoke about how separate those communities were. Savoy needed an outlet to figure out how to use his voice in a way that mattered. He looked beyond the traditional classroom to ask these questions. He thrived in the non-formal education environment. During the second year of the fellowship, he participated in our social justice curriculum. Our ECYP youth partner with a group of Jewish teens to examine the history of Black and white Jewish experiences in Baltimore and explore social justice issues in their backyards. Recently, participants worked together to produce a podcast on housing justice in Maryland, gaining the confidence to interview and to be in conversation with local and state officials on topics that matter to them.

We provide youth like Savoy with the skills and knowledge to continue to use tools that enable them to be leaders in their community. In the spring of his sophomore year at Loyola University Maryland, Savoy wrote to the administration when he saw a void in Black history being taught in a school that is rooted in a city with a population of over 60% Black people. He pressed the administration to do better and provide more opportunities to learn about Black history. He also started a club called Addressing the System to call attention to systemic injustices on campus and in Baltimore City. Savoy is only at the start of his journey, but he is truly living the legacy of the Congressman.

As a community educator with ECYP, I work alongside young people like Savoy in Maryland's Seventh District to connect them with people who are similar and dissimilar to their lived experiences. The outside-school-time, non-formal environment is expansive and allows for opportunities to engage young people in dialogue and opportunities that is sometimes difficult in formal education spaces. I see formal and non-formal educational spaces as places of synergy. I stumbled upon this work after graduating from college. I was hired to be a facilitator for students across the country who came to Washington DC. We used the city as a living classroom to connect young people with the idea of civics and citizenship responsibilities. Almost two decades later, I am still steeped in this work. With ECYP, I continue to invite young people to imagine how they can use the spaces that they walk into as learning spaces, in Baltimore and in Israel. Out-of-school learning, education outside of the classroom, is essential to cultivating well-rounded and open-minded citizens. This helps students explore who they are as young leaders in relation to communities that are different than their own. The outcome of this work leads to students building diverse and global relationships with teens.

Congressman Elijah Cummings' death in October 2019 was a tremendous loss for our community and the nation. He had been a formidable figure, not only in Maryland, but also on the national stage. He had a booming voice that could quiet a room. He was passionate about public service and offering opportunities for young people in his district. Two years before his death, Congressman Elijah Cummings said, "When I look back at my life, if there is anything that I am most proud, the thing I want my legacy to be about is this program." We who keep it going in his absence continue to create opportunities for non-formal, extracurricular learning so that young people like Savoy may build relationships and bridges within and beyond their communities.

## FOR REFLECTION

1  How might out-of-school-time programming provide added learning opportunities for students?

2  Consider your own local religious history. How can you use it to illuminate the current religious landscape where you live for your students?

3  Congressman Cummings left a legacy of bridge-building. What communities might your students need to engage in order to build bridges?

# NOTES

1. Council of Europe, "Linguistic Integration of Adult Migrants: Formal, non-formal, and informal learning," www.coe.int.

2. Reservoir Hill holds an important place in Baltimore's Jewish history. Anchored by two synagogues, the neighborhood was a Jewish cultural hub and place for both Baltimore's German Jewish and eastern European Jewish communities to come together in the early twentieth century. Following the Jewish population's move into the surrounding suburbs and counties and a continued history of red-lining and blockbusting, Black Baltimoreans moved into the neighborhood. Today, Black residents and Jewish residents live side by side. For an in-depth history of these communities, see Eric L. Goldstein and Deborah R. Weiner, *On Middle Ground: A History of the Jews of Baltimore* (Baltimore: Johns Hopkins University Press, 2018).

# 17

# INTERFAITH BRIDGES FROM HIGH SCHOOL TO COLLEGE
## The Key Learning Goals of Interfaith Pre-Orientation Programs

*Gregory W. McGonigle*

The transition from high school to college is one of the most significant moments in many students' lives. Simultaneously, many things change for many students, especially those who move to attend a residential college. In this rite of passage, students leave behind their high school and, often, their high school friends; they leave behind their home community, sometimes including a faith community; and they transition into a new relationship with their family as they become increasingly independent and responsible for more aspects of their day-to-day lives and choices. At the same time, they have an opportunity to refine and reshape their identities, and they become part of a new community that encourages them to identify their unique academic interests, their personal passions, the people they will choose to associate with, the groups they will join, and in a significant way, the experiences and values that will shape their personal lives and careers for the future.

For many students in the past, this transition to college has involved a traditional college orientation—often filled with information sessions on academic honor codes and residential life rules and regulations; a smorgasbord of open houses and resource fairs; tasks like getting an ID card, registering for classes, buying books, and finding one's way around; and, usually, some social activities and historic traditions. Over the past number of years, many colleges and universities have realized that this transition is so significant that it deserves more time and care, and that establishing friendships and a good social network with compatible peers is one of the most important parts of this transition for students' wellbeing and overall success. In light of this, at many universities, pre-orientation programs have emerged, creating a space where incoming students with common interests can share a common experience before they have all the requirements of academics and student jobs and other activities—a space in which they may simply explore, build friendships, and create a foundation for their life as well as their learning. Popular among these programs are ones that involve camping trips in the wilderness and sometimes fitness-related programs as well. More recently, other programs centering on interests and identities that incoming students share have been developed.

When I became University Chaplain at Tufts University in 2013, I learned of such a program that had been sponsored by the Tufts University Chaplaincy for interfaith learning and engagement. It was called the CAFE program (an acronym for "Conversation, Action, Faith, and Education"), and it had been developed by chaplains and some students through a Department of Defense grant made available after September 11, 2001. The program had been offered a handful of times with ten or fewer students participating. In terms of creating a culture of interfaith engagement and a positive climate for religious and philosophical diversity and learning, I sensed that this kind of opportunity would offer many benefits on many levels both for the student participants and for the university at large. If the program could be curated by the University Chaplaincy with such learning goals in mind, then the opportunity would increase.

And so, working with our multifaith chaplaincy team and a group of interested students, we decided to renew and re-launch the CAFE program as a weeklong immersive pre-orientation program focused on religious diversity in interfaith engagement. In a short time, it became a program that would regularly draw up to fifty students per year between the student coordinators, peer leaders, and the incoming students who participated in the program—a perfect number given the size of many of the faith communities we would visit in the program. Many of the students would come to say that it was one of the most transformative experiences of their undergraduate education because of several of the features that were built into the program.

When I became Dean of Religious Life at Emory University in 2019, the project I could bring there that was most compelling to students, faculty, and staff was the development of an interfaith pre-orientation program. In my second academic year, even during the COVID-19 pandemic, we were able to launch a pre-orientation program for first-year students. This program is called WISE—"Welcoming Interfaith and Spiritual Exploration." The acronym draws on the Emory motto, "The wise heart seeks knowledge" (Proverbs 15:14).

In what follows, my reflections draw upon both the Tufts CAFE and the Emory WISE programs. I describe some of the key features of interfaith pre-orientation programs as a bridge between secondary school and college. I discuss six main features of these programs as learning goals, and the ways that they benefit both individual participants and the larger culture of the university campus: social-emotional learning, interfaith leadership, religious and philosophical literacy, social justice education, wellness practices, and the shaping of the campus climate.

This essay was written during the period in which we were preparing for the second iteration of WISE (August 2022), which we assumed would build upon some of the insights we learned from the first. Such is the adaptability of these programs to develop over time, striving to best meet the various educational and campus climate-related goals. Interfaith pre-orientation programs have tremendous potential both for equipping individual students as interfaith leaders and for creating university climates that are marked by the value of interfaith engagement. And we hope in doing so, these programs have positive personal and institutional influences for peace in our larger society and world.

## Program Description

To begin, it may be helpful to offer a brief outline of an interfaith pre-orientation program and the steps involved in its planning. I owe a great debt to Zachary Cole, who serves as my chief of staff at Emory (and before that, at Tufts) and brings a strong higher education administration background into the work of university spiritual life. Best practices emerging from higher education administration and general orientation program development have been critical to the success of developing and implementing both the CAFE and WISE pre-orientation programs. Likewise, our dedicated student leaders, and especially the initial student coordinators of both programs, were vital to building the programs and making them successful.

In many ways Tufts and Emory are similar schools, both being private national research universities with similar religious demographics. In recent years, both schools have been in the process of renewing their focus on the undergraduate experience, beginning with orientation and pre-orientation programs. Some differences to note are that Tufts is located in the Northeast near Boston, Massachusetts and has about 5,800 undergraduates, whereas Emory is located in the South near Atlanta, Georgia with about 8,200 undergraduates. Emory was founded in 1836 by the Methodist Episcopal Church and it maintains a historical affiliation with the United Methodist Church. Tufts was founded in 1852 by the Universalist Church and has become nonsectarian over time. Both universities have a multifaith chaplaincy program.

Both have developed a consistent focus on interfaith engagement and leadership development over the past thirty years.

Both interfaith pre-orientation programs began with a small group of committed student leaders who worked with our multifaith university chaplaincy team to plan these programs. Our staff met with these student leaders to collaboratively sketch out a vision for the programs that would meet the six key learning goals I will discuss below. After this initial visioning, the student planners became the student coordinators of the programs, which became a kind of spring and summer internship for them (part-time in the spring, and full-time in summer and during the pre-orientation programs themselves).

One of the student coordinators' first spring tasks was to help select a group of ten or so student peer leaders to be the main counselors in the programs. This was done through applications and interviews. Once those peer leaders were selected and trained, they became ambassadors for the programs and the counselors to help to facilitate the program content. The student coordinators were generally selected in January and February, and they selected the peer leader group in March and April. We sought to select a peer leader group that was diverse in multiple ways religiously, racially, and in terms of gender and sexual orientation in order to help provide an inclusive leadership team for the programs. Some initial gatherings and orientations were then offered for the ten or so peer leaders before the summer break. Then, in the two or three days just before the programs in August, a more intensive training was offered for the coordinators and peer leaders involving the outline and logistics of the programs, skill-building in group facilitation, and important information the universities wanted all pre-orientation leaders to have, including resources for mental health referrals, sexual misconduct referrals, and so forth.

As offers of admission were made to new students in April and May, our office would coordinate with the university admissions and orientation offices to offer the interfaith pre-orientation programs to accepted incoming students as an opportunity. Students had a period of time to enroll in the programs, and our office then communicated with those who were accepted throughout the summer until the programs began in August. Both institutions decided to make the programs free or as affordable as possible for incoming students for reasons of economic justice and to help facilitate registration in the programs.

The student coordinators worked over the summer to help frame out the logistics of the programs. Both programs were approximately one week long, and we sought to include the major religious gatherings that take place on Friday with Jum'ah and Shabbat as part of the schedule. At Tufts, Christian Sunday worship services were also included, whereas at Emory, a Wednesday night Christian Bible study and Christian music concert were included.

Generally, on the first day of the programs, students moved in and were greeted with icebreakers and introductions to their small groups led by the peer leaders before a welcome dinner, followed by an overview of the week, developing of community guidelines, and an activity of sharing their spiritual journeys. The programs always began with a session on sharing our spiritual journeys as a way for the students to get to know one another and to be grounded in the idea of being on a spiritual journey. These might be religious, spiritual, or humanistic journeys, and students would portray them as a timeline with art or with words.

The successive days of the programs involved breakfast and orientations to the day ahead, community visits to various spiritual communities (variously Native American, Hindu, Buddhist, Jewish, Christian, Muslim, Sikh, and Humanist), as well as leadership development sessions on social justice, civic engagement, and wellness practices.

As University Chaplain, I generally led the initial session on spiritual journeys and offered a session on the first morning about religious diversity and pluralism, interfaith leadership, and the ethics of community visits. Because the core of the programs involved our visits to various religious and philosophical communities in the city locations of our campuses, we felt it was important to reflect on the ethics of forming relationships with these communities. We encourage the students to think about not being tourists on site visits but building relationships with faith communities as neighbors. To facilitate that, we encouraged them to learn about the histories and programs of the various spiritual communities, to be conscious and respectful in their presence there, and to ask good questions of the hosts who greeted us at each center. To facilitate their learning about the histories of the spiritual communities we visited, we offered informational handouts in the students' orientation folders and held discussions led by the chaplains and peer leaders in advance about what the participants might experience.

Throughout each day of the programs, usually in the morning, at midday, and in the evening, the peer leaders would lead small group discussions as check-ins and debriefing times with their students. We also sought to incorporate throughout the programs meals with delicious food to model promoting health in body, mind, and spirit. Over time, we added in more sessions for wellness and self-care, often led by the peer leaders, in which they would lead movement practices or walks in favorite places around the campus or meditation sessions or perhaps a trip to the fitness center. We would also invite to the programs various important leaders whom we wanted to introduce to the students, including the university president, vice presidents and deans, chairs of the Religion and other relevant academic departments, and leaders in important areas of campus life such as civic engagement and the multicultural resource centers.

In addition, in both programs we offered several leadership development sessions on social justice including awareness of identities such as race, gender, sexual orientation, and religion and an introduction to the concepts of power, privilege, oppression, and allyship. We also incorporated a session on civic and community engagement to encourage students to find their place to give back as members of the community. And we sought to end each program with a ritual that was a kind of a highpoint for the students. At Tufts in Boston with the CAFE program, it was a harbor cruise in Boston which became a beautiful way to conclude. At Emory, it was an affirmation circle after the Shabbat dinner on Friday night.

These programs included site visits. Possibilities included puja at a Hindu temple, a Sikh gurdwara—where we enjoyed langar (community meal)—a Buddhist center at which we might participate in a meditation or work in the monastery, a Jewish Shabbat service and dinner, a "choose your own adventure" Christian worship or Bible study experience, Jum'ah prayer at the mosque, and, when possible, a visit to a Humanist center. At Tufts, we also included a site visit to the Royall House and Slave Quarters museum, which is an important site for learning about the history of enslavement in the United States and especially in the North. At Emory, we visited the Atlanta History Center and exhibit on Native Lands to learn more about the Muscogee Creek and Cherokee peoples—on whose ancestral territory Emory's campuses are located.

In addition, both programs sought to introduce students to the campus itself and to help them get oriented even before their main orientation began. And both programs developed some of their own follow-up experiences. At Tufts, it became a student organization spinoff called COFFEE, which was an interest group where alumni of the CAFE program could continue to engage in interfaith dialogue and exploration. At Emory, it became a first-year seminar called Emory Edge, co-led by our Hindu and Buddhist Chaplains, as an extension of the main orientation program.

The multifaith chaplaincy teams at each university offered introductions to their religious traditions and served as guides to the spiritual communities we visited. Where we had student peer leaders who were part of the traditions whose sacred sites we were visiting, they also shared their experiences of growing up in the various faith communities we visited.

In terms of budget, the highest expenses of the programs were generally food and transportation. The total budget was approximately $30,000 for the week. At both universities, students were permitted to move into their residence halls early without additional charges, which greatly facilitated access to the programs. And we offered honoraria to the various speakers we invited to lead and to the communities we visited as signs of our appreciation. In both programs, students created a T-shirt that we gave to the participants, and we also had banners, stickers, and pins to help raise visibility of the programs. The students were also provided with a university chaplaincy water bottle that became their water source for meals and visits throughout the programs. But otherwise, supplies were minimal, consisting mostly of the art supplies needed for various activities such as mapping our spiritual journeys activity.

After the programs, we would send the leaders and participants an evaluation so that we would be able to continue to improve the programs year to year. We thanked the leaders with a group photo from the programs, and the cohorts of leaders and participants became a network that the university chaplaincies could return to and involve in all manner of interfaith programming, dialogues, service opportunities, and many other opportunities for service to the campus.

The programs became a wonderful way for the students involved to become settled at their new campus, to make new friends with common interests, to increase their religious and interfaith literacy skills, to learn about opportunities to support their wellness, to learn about opportunities for continuing leadership and service, and to be part of shaping a campus culture that was supportive of religious diversity and interfaith engagement.

## Learning Goals

The CAFE and WISE interfaith pre-orientation programs were intended to advance at least six key learning goals, and the weaving together of these goals and their interaction helped to create programs that are transformative for the student experience. These goals are social-emotional learning, interfaith leadership, religious literacy, social justice awareness, wellness, and positive impact on campus climate. In what follows, I discuss how the programs embodied and promoted each of these learning goals.

Social-emotional learning has been defined by the Collaborative for Academic, Social, and Emotional Learning (CASEL) as the development of the knowledge, skills, and attitudes to form healthy identities and relationships and to make caring and responsible impacts on larger communities.[1] In that framework, it involves five key aspects: self-awareness, self-management, social awareness, relationship skills, and responsible decision-making. While the interfaith pre-orientation programs do not address each of these areas in an explicit way, the culture of the programs is intended to support the development of these competencies.

We recognize that most of the incoming student participants come into the programs at a period of great transition in their lives—moving from family, academic, and home communities, and sometimes faith communities, into the residential experiences of our campuses. In light of that, we seek to create an environment that is safe, healthy, and just, marked by trust, collaboration, learning, and growth. The student coordinators and peer leaders, under the overall guidance of our multifaith chaplaincy team, are charged with facilitating this transition for the students involved. The presence of chaplains throughout the programs in different ways allows us to be a supportive presence to the students at a significant time of personal development.

In addition, we recruit student coordinators and peer leaders that we believe will help create a caring and supportive environment for first-year students. The coordinators and peer leaders develop covenants of community guidelines with one another about how they will serve as leaders and mentors to the incoming students. They are charged with creating a welcoming environment from the first moments the student participants prepare to come to campus and move in. The peer leaders do things such as decorate the residence hall doors of the incoming students to help them know that they are deeply welcomed. They lead icebreakers and small group conversations, and they continue to extend this environment of care and encourage the values of self-awareness, self-management, social awareness, relationship skills, and responsible decision-making.

On the first night of the programs, when the incoming students are welcomed, they are invited to create a covenant of community guidelines with one another about how they will conduct themselves throughout the programs. This creates a supportive environment in which the students may transition, learn, and grow while expressing their needs and hopes. We also try to be caring and supportive of students throughout the programs by offering nutritious and delicious food at meals and opportunities for recreation and rest as well as support for their spiritual identities and cultural practices so that they feel emotionally and socially cared for and able to participate fully in the programs. As important as the content of our programs is, we want the culture of the programs itself to be our primary learning goal and to communicate the ethics that we hope students will carry with them throughout their relationships and time at the university.

The second major learning goal of the programs is interfaith leadership. After students have an opportunity to reflect on, express, and describe their own spiritual journeys to one another in small groups on the first night of the programs, the next morning I host a session on the topic of religious diversity and pluralism, interfaith leadership, and the ethics of community partnerships. Students generally choose to do the interfaith pre-orientation programs because they want to explore religious diversity and think about the potential of interfaith leadership, but they may or may not have had the opportunity to deeply consider concepts such as religious diversity and pluralism before they come to the university. Our theoretical framework is grounded in the work of the Pluralism Project at Harvard University, which sees religious diversity as a fact and pluralism as an achievement, brought about by engagement, understanding, and relationships between people of different faiths and philosophies.[2] We teach this framework and our belief in the values of interfaith engagement for individual lives, for our campus community, and for the larger society and world.

In light of this, we encourage students to think of themselves as interfaith leaders and to develop the knowledge, the skills, and the qualities to claim that role. In teaching about this, we draw upon the theoretical work of Eboo Patel in *Interfaith Leadership: A Primer*, discussing the kinds of skills and relationships that they may need to develop to live into their roles as interfaith leaders.[3] And because the programs are rooted in community partnerships and visits, we also discuss the ethics of visiting and interacting with spiritual communities. I was formed in this work by my own research with the Harvard Pluralism Project, which encouraged me to be reflective about my own identities and the purposes for which I was relating with the spiritual communities I was studying, as well as the mutuality that should be present in these ideally sustainable human relationships. In the programs, we seek to help students understand that making community visits creates relationships and responsibilities, and that we seek to be good allies with our religious neighbors, conscious of our role as part of a research university.

The next learning goal of course is that of religious literacy itself, which we see as an important competency for one to be an effective interfaith leader. Of course, religions and philosophies are numerous, vast, and deep, and no one program will introduce students to all manifestations of even one religious community, nor can we be fully comprehensive of many. Nevertheless, we seek to provide a baseline knowledge of some of the major spiritual traditions they will encounter on campus as a template for how they can continue their lifelong learning. Rooted as we are in our regions, we seek to start with the lifeways of the Native Peoples of our areas so that our students can be mindful of the First Nations and cultures of the land of their campuses and their ongoing presence and perspectives. We have then visited a series of religious and philosophical communities, at each community welcomed at the invitation of hosts who guide us and teach us and help us to learn. An important aspect of these visits is a focus on "lived religion"—although we discuss doctrines and beliefs and laws, we encourage students to see this as an opportunity to really witness how religious traditions are practiced by their adherents, whether or not that always corresponds with every official belief or scriptural teaching. We ask our hosts personally about their spiritual journeys and what is most important to them about their traditions. We also encourage students to have an appreciation for sacred spaces, as many of the communities we visit are housed in beautiful sanctuaries and holy places. This is an opportunity to attend to the aesthetic dimension of religions in architecture, art, and music, and we hope to set the students on a journey of discovery in the realm of human spirituality for their lives. As participants have reported in their evaluations of the program, this has also encouraged them to explore their own traditions more deeply as well.

An intimately related learning goal is that of social justice awareness and education. In our interfaith pre-orientation programs, we do not teach religious traditions as separated from human beings and from human history and from the legacies of power, privilege, and oppression, but rather, we seek to present religion and spirituality as part of a quest for human wholeness, liberation, equality, and justice. Therefore, we think it is crucial to introduce students, especially as they aspire to become leaders (if they have not already been introduced), to concepts of social justice. We discuss concepts of race, ethnicity, gender, sexual orientation, class, and other identities that interact with religion and philosophy in complex ways for students to see linked nature of oppressions and the opportunities for liberation. We hope that in their own ways, whether as part of religious traditions or not, they will become leaders whose work is marked by an awareness of diversity, equity, inclusion, and social justice, by deep empathy for others, and by caring for their wellbeing and supporting their needs and interests as effective allies.

In addition to the learning goals of religious literacy and social justice, we see wellness practices as critical for incoming students to develop, not only to be successful students and leaders, but also to flourish in life generally, especially if they take up the mantle of social justice work and interfaith leadership longer-term. We know that practices of wellbeing are crucial in order to sustain those efforts over time. We affirm that practices of relaxation and rest, contemplation and reflection, creativity and inspiration are vital to a life well lived. We encourage especially our peer leaders to teach and model the practices that they employ to help them find centeredness and well-being and grounding in their lives. For some students, it may be prayer practices, meditation, congregational worship, yoga, fitness practices, walking, journaling, crafts, or music—many different sorts of outlets are possible for advancing the learning goal of holistic wellness. But whatever the form, especially given the rising numbers of students today expressing experiences with anxiety and depression, we know that practices of wellness are essential to their being and staying healthy in their lives.

The final and overall learning goal for the entire interfaith pre-orientation programs is that of shaping a pluralistic campus climate. While this is not necessarily an individual learning goal for each student, collectively interfaith pre-orientation programs create communities within the programs, and as the student participants later disperse throughout the campus, they help the campus to become marked by increased religious pluralism and interfaith engagement. In this way, the programs become not insular and isolated but ones that have a transformative impact on the ecology of the campus overall, encouraging people to bring forward their identities with authenticity, integrity, respect, and care and to make space as allies for the deepest and most sacred beliefs, practices, and values of their neighbors. We have seen this take shape in the student organization that alumni of the program at Tufts created; we have seen it also in a first-year seminar course that the Emory chaplains led. In less structured ways, the alumni of the pre-orientation programs have gone on to become involved in campus interfaith councils and in their own spiritual communities, in service projects and dialogue groups and student governments, in ways that advance a culture of peacemaking in connection with spiritual and cultural traditions. As our students take next steps in their studies and their careers, we see that the programs have met the ultimate learning goals of shaping them into connected and caring leaders, and hopefully shaping a campus and a world that is marked by interfaith respect and cooperation.

## CONCLUSION

In conclusion, interfaith pre-orientation programs can be highly effective immersive experiences for meeting some of the crucial developmental goals of the life transition between high school and college, and the developmental goals of forming interfaith leaders who are marked by religious literacy, social justice, wellness practices, and a sense of responsibility for their larger communities. Having taught world religions at a private secondary school, I can also see how some of these aspects and learning goals could be taught in the curriculum or co-curriculum at the secondary school level. In addition, as a Unitarian Universalist minister, I am aware that there have for many years been curricula in my own tradition's religious education programs that have encouraged learning about neighboring faiths and building a culture of respect, mutual learning, and cooperation among faith communities.[4] This is likely true of other faith traditions as well, and it could indeed be so in other youth organizations that might even choose to highlight particular interfaith themes or questions—such as environmentalism, or addressing racial justice, or supporting LGBTQ people across faiths. These programs are adaptable; but developed intentionally, they are so much more than simple tours to different faith traditions' houses of worship. They can and should be opportunities for self-development and reflection, relationship building, social development, and consciousness-raising to the challenges and opportunities facing our religiously diverse world. Programs like these offer an excellent opportunity to develop interfaith leaders who will go on to lead with respect and appreciation for the beliefs and values of others and awareness of how they can work together with others for the common good.[5]

## FOR REFLECTION

1    How might programs like CAFE or WISE be experienced differently by a student from a historically privileged religious identity vs. a historically marginalized religious identity? What might need to be changed about the programs to center such a perspective?

2    Occasionally in programs like CAFE or WISE, some of the deep fault lines within and between faith communities over political issues may emerge—perspectives on the Middle East, for example, or on abortion or LGBTQ issues. How could such programs meaningfully address these debates and dialogues? Should they be built in?

3    CAFE and WISE are programs for new college and university students, but some private secondary schools and faith or community organizations might offer similar programs to build religious literacy and interfaith leadership. How might such programs be adapted differently for those settings? How might they be incorporated into youth leadership development? What might need to be adapted about these programs for a youth group?

# NOTES

1. Collaborative for Academic, Social, and Emotional Learning, https://casel.org.

2. The Pluralism Project at Harvard University, https://pluralism.org.

3. Eboo Patel, *Interfaith Leadership: A Primer* (Boston: Beacon Press, 2016).

4. Dan Harper, "Neighboring Faith Communities," *Yet Another UU Curriculum Site.*

5. When developing a program, the following resources (in addition to those cited above) may be helpful: Diana L. Eck, *A New Religious America: How a "Christian Country" Has Become the World's Most Religiously Diverse Nation* (San Francisco: Harper, 2002); Stuart M. Matlins and Arthur J. Magida, eds. *How to Be a Perfect Stranger: The Essential Religious Etiquette Handbook* (Nashville, TN: SkyLight Paths, 2006); Stephen Prothero, *Religious Literacy: What Every American Needs to Know—And Doesn't* (San Francisco: HarperOne, 2008).

# AFTERWORD

# TEACHERS AND PREACHERS
## The Contested Role of Educators in the Classroom

*Heather Miller Rubens*

In 1925, the Scopes Monkey Trial gripped the United States.[1] Could a public-school teacher instruct students about evolution—a scientific theory that seemingly challenged a biblical account of creation? Tennessee had just passed a state law prohibiting the teaching of lessons that denied the divine creation of humanity.[2] John T. Scopes, a small-town science teacher, was charged with violating this law by teaching the theories of Charles Darwin.[3] William Jennings Bryan and Clarence Darrow—two celebrity politician-attorneys—squared off in the courtroom, engaging in debates over how theology, science, and biblical interpretation should impact the education of America's children. News reporters, having been sent from around the country to cover the sensational trial, gave birth to a dynamic with which we remain familiar: the deeming of certain kinds of knowledge as dangerous and the casting of teachers as agents of indoctrination who are threats, not only to the children in their classrooms, but also to the very fabric of society. Classrooms became proxy battlefields in a broader cultural war. Teachers were placed on trial. Classroom activities were watched closely by parents, attacked by the media, and regulated by the courts and local government.

Ninety-nine years later, culture wars still roil. Arguments over what students should be learning and how teachers should be teaching continue apace. In the American imagination, teachers themselves become particularly dangerous figures when they touch upon religion and ethics in their classrooms. Hence, from their vantage points outside secondary school classroom walls, coalitions of parents advocate for book bans and religious exemptions from health and sexual education curriculum; media speculate that "woke" teachers are indoctrinating the next generation with new interpretative theories and divisive texts; and state legislatures and courts alternate between curtailing teachers' freedom to explore hard histories and empowering teachers to pray publicly at school with their students.

But what is actually happening inside America's secondary school classrooms? In some, there is innovative engagement with religious and moral diversity. *Interreligious Studies and Secondary Education: Pedagogies and Practices for Living and Learning in a Religiously Plural World* has provided a window on such possibilities. This volume can be a valuable "how-to" resource. However, it is more than that. I see in it an invitation to educators to undertake thoughtful reconsideration of their own important (and contested) position in this work. The role of the teacher remains under scrutiny. The U.S. courts have had a major role in shaping the ongoing conversation on the appropriate role of teachers. Furthermore, the courts themselves have been impacted by the evolving public conversation on the appropriate government regulation of religion in schools and in public institutions. Against the backdrop of America's evolving interpretation of the role religion should play in public life, teachers find themselves impacted by legal decisions and popular media narratives. As the foundations and the aims of religious education are challenged and contested in society, the roles teachers can and should play are reevaluated and renegotiated. How might this be done? I suggest that we revisit this volume's seventeen essays by means of a paradigm drawing upon key U. S. Supreme Court decisions that have had a bearing on how teachers engage in education around religion and religious diversity.

## THE TEACHER CANNOT BE A PREAZCHER: THE LEGACY OF *ABINGTON V SCHEMPP* (1963)

*Abington v Schempp* made a distinction between "teaching religion" and "teaching about religion." It argued that, while "teaching religion" was not permitted in public school contexts, "teaching about religion" was allowed.[4] During the sixty years since, teachers—particularly in K–12 public schools—have had almost no guidance about what they can and cannot "teach about religion" in their classrooms. Each teacher has a vague sense of the First Amendment boundaries summed up in one sentence by the court (and subsequently adopted by the Department of Education): "Public schools may not provide religious instruction, but they may teach about religion." In the humanities, "religion" may be taught as it relates to something else—philosophy, history, literature, art, music, and social studies. And certain religious teachings are often unspoken adversaries to education in the hard sciences, social sciences, and health curriculums in many schools. In this regard, the U.S. Department of Education acknowledges a problem that public school teachers have been experiencing in their classrooms: religion is both everywhere and nowhere, within a K–12 curriculum. Yet most people have presumed that the "Wall of Separation" kept religion out of public-school classrooms. There are many who believe that in its 1963 opinion *Abington School District v. Schempp*, "the [U. S.] Supreme Court, like the God of Genesis, came down and created separation. Earth from sky, land from water; the teaching of religion from teaching about religion."[5] What does "teaching about religion" mean exactly? And how do everyday teachers interpret this guidance?

If public school teachers are not preachers, but are tasked instead with "teaching about religion" to their students, what possible roles can they inhabit with their students? Authors focused on American public-school contexts offer a few choices worth noting. "Not-Preacher" teachers in an *Abington* legal framework can: 1) teach religions through cultural studies, 2) serve as local tour guides and translators at various houses of worship, or 3) be intellectual historians and theorists.

John Camardella favors the move many social studies teachers have made from a world-religions and traditions-based approach to a cultural-studies and case-based approach. The teacher is not a preacher in these modalities, but rather the teacher serves as a guide to students, with cultural studies providing the framework for "teaching about religion."

Christopher Murphy augments a primarily text-based cultural studies model with a "lived religions" / cultural anthropology approach. He observes that a "lived religions" approach allows students to experience direct engagement of the religious diversity of their communities through class visits to houses of worship. This methodology allows for religious people to speak for themselves during these student visits. The teacher functions as a tour guide, providing translations and explanations for students directly engaged with their local religious diversity. The "lived religions" model works especially well in religiously diverse communities like Maryland's Montgomery County (in the Washington, DC suburbs) where Murphy teaches.

John Shekitka argues that teachers can successfully take an intellectual-history approach to the contested definition of religion, using philosophers and theorists as the principal guides to a classroom exploration of religion. All of these suggested models attempt to "teach about religion" rather than "teach religion" in the public-school setting; all seek to reimagine what roles teachers can/should inhabit in their classrooms. But if teachers can't be preachers with their students, have teacher-preachers been fully removed from public schools? Vicki Scullion argues that this has *not* been the legacy of *Abington*. Implicitly, Scullion suggests a broader frame than teacher-student, that an appropriate legacy of *Abington* is a commitment to reject Christian Supremacy in American public schools, including internal faculty relations at public schools. From this starting presupposition, she then explores experiences of non-Christian faculty in Georgia public schools, arguing that many Christian teachers are often behaving like preachers with their non-Christian colleagues.

## THE TEACHER IS A PREACHER:
## THE LEGACY OF *HOSANNA-TABOR EVANGELICAL LUTHERAN CHURCH AND SCHOOL V. EEOC* (2012)

With *Hosanna-Tabor Evangelical Lutheran Church and School v. EEOC* (2012), the U.S. Supreme Court gave religiously affiliated schools in the United States broad authority and ability to hire and fire teachers. Adopting a robust interpretation of the "ministerial exception" to the Civil Rights Act of 1964, the Supreme Court justices unanimously determined that the First Amendment prohibits government from being involved with the employment matters of religious institutions, including religious schools. As Chief Justice John Roberts wrote, "the Establishment Clause prevents the Government from appointing ministers, and the Free Exercise clause prevents it from interfering with the freedom of religious groups to select their own."[6] Thus teachers in religious schools in the United States find their guidance for both "teaching religion" and "teaching about religion" from their respective school administrators, religious denominations, and ecclesial authorities.

In this schema, the religious school teacher is a preacher.[7] What is their experience with "teaching religion" and "teaching about religion"? In *Interreligious Studies and Secondary Education*, we hear from three educators working within Roman Catholic schools who are creatively negotiating the resources available within the Roman Catholic tradition to both "teach Catholicism" and "teach about other religions." Notably, all the authors are seeking ways to be accountable to their Catholic communities and to Catholic teachings, while also being conscious of the demographic reality that most American Catholic schools today have a sizeable number of non-Catholic students and staff. While these essays all draw from teacher experiences in Catholic schools, readers can glean broader lessons on both the challenges and opportunities that may arise for educators teaching at religious schools.

In these particular essays, the language is not quite "teacher as preacher." Rather, it takes on a Catholic idiom—"the teacher as catechist."[8] Importantly, as scholars and theorists consider the various ways in which teachers within different religious institutional contexts negotiate their "ministerial" obligations, the particular language and concepts of each religious community should inform scholarly reflection. In *Interreligious Studies and Secondary Education*, we have met authors who—as they have negotiated a Catholic worldview in an American context—have explored the idea that the Catholic school teacher is a catechist. As is popularly understood by America's Catholic school teachers, a catechist is someone who has an obligation "simply" to present students with Church teachings and dogma. Chase de Saint-Felix describes this as the default position among his faculty colleagues at a Catholic school. They contend that the Church has clear teachings, and their central obligation as teachers in a Catholic school is to present their students with the correct information about Church dogma. De Saint-Felix critiques the simplicity of this position, arguing instead that such a position does not take into account the lived realities of American Catholicism, nor does it acknowledge the diverse needs of the students. By means of his two rules for the theology classroom, de Saint-Felix offers a way for teachers to present Church teachings while also making intentional room for lived religion and religious diversity.[9] In his suggested schema, the teacher-catechist is not simply a conduit for dogma. The teacher-catechist is a guide in facilitating student reflection on the dynamic realities of dogma and practice, Church authority and individual conscience. David Michael Avram Gregory takes the critique of a catechetical mindset in the classroom even further. He posits a creative alternative to the Catholic catechetical model—using both secular and Catholic sources—that imagines the classroom as a place where existentially meaningful conversations happen, facilitated by teachers who are trying to help sustain students on their respective spiritual journeys. Brendan O'Kane makes the compelling argument that creating an interreligious classroom is part of Catholic tradition and teachings. This work is not external to Catholicism, nor is it a fashionable educational fad being imposed on Catholic schools from outside, as some Catholic school parents might fear. Rather, as O'Kane highlights, there exist abundant theological, conceptual, and practical resources within the Catholic tradition for interreligious engagement. In excavating and enumerating the available Catholic sources that support educators in Catholic schools to create interreligious classrooms, O'Kane's imagined teacher is recast as a humble Catholic preacher capable and ready to foster interreligious learning and dialogue in a Catholic style.

All these educators are working within a Hosanna-Tabor legal framework—which means taking seriously their job to "teach religion" according to the religious tradition of their school and to "teach about other religions" in ways that do not demean or diminish other religions. These essays show the creative work was happening in a Catholic context; but one can imagine teachers working at other religious institutions mining their own traditions to do this important work. It is important that scholars need to attend to the particularities of such diverse projects.

## TEACHERS' SPEECH RIGHTS AND PERSONAL RELIGIOUS IDENTITY: THE LEGACY OF *KENNEDY V. BREMERTON SCHOOL DISTRICT* (2022)

With its decision on *Kennedy v. Bremerton School District* (2022), the U.S. Supreme Court affirmed the free speech and religious exercise rights of public school teachers, asserting that they did not lose those rights when they entered classrooms or football fields. Nearly sixty years after *Abington v. Schempp* asked public school teachers to suppress their personal religiosity in the classroom, *Kennedy v. Bremerton School District* (2022) brought the religiosity of teachers back into the conversation.

In short, in this case, Joseph Kennedy, a football coach working for a public high school in Bremerton, Washington (across Puget Sound from Seattle) had been engaging regularly in Christian prayer with students during and after football games. His employer demanded that he stop this practice, asserting that the coach's actions violated the Establishment Clause of the First Amendment, as interpreted by *Abington v. Schempp*. Coach Kennedy sued the school district, arguing that the school district had violated his personal rights to free speech and to religious freedom, as protected by the First Amendment and the Civil Rights Act of 1964. The Supreme Court ruled in favor of Coach Kennedy, with Justice Neil Gorsuch writing: "Both the Free Exercise and Free Speech Clauses of the First Amendment protect expressions like Mr. Kennedy's...The Constitution and the best of our traditions counsel mutual respect and tolerance, not censorship and suppression, for religious and nonreligious views alike."[10] If, before Kennedy, public school teachers were keeping their personal religiosity under wraps, after Kennedy, the religious freedoms of teachers have once again come into the conversation.

Among the essays in the present volume that report on the best engagement of this "new" dynamic are some from educators working in independent and private schools. Independent-school teachers have been impacted differently by *Abington &*

*Hosanna-Tabor*, escaping the "teacher is/is not a preacher" binary. Operating in a liminal space between public and religious education, independent school teachers are the ones who have most robustly interrogated and problematized the religious identity and positionality of the teacher and the place of religious practice in the classroom. Eleni Lampadarios and Travis Henschen, both of whom teach in a Quaker school, engage in self-reflective and self-critical assessments about how their own religious identities impact their approach to interreligious education. Lampadarios reflects on her experience as a practicing Orthodox Christian who has been learning and teaching in different American Christian contexts throughout her life. She values liturgical experiences in both Quaker Meeting for Worship and Taizé prayer, asserting that these opportunities have deepened her appreciation for Orthodox Christian worship and strengthened her religious identity. Using Krister Stendhal's concept of "holy envy" as a guide, Lampadarios invites her students to cultivate an openness to new religious experiences while at the same time appreciating the spiritual heritage they hold. Travis Henschen identifies as a "religious none" and persuasively argues that teachers can and should bring their non-religious/religiously-unaffiliated/secular identities into the broader conversation about religion in the classroom. As the number of people who are religiously unaffiliated continues to grow, this important demographic must be included in the development of pedagogies and practices that support religious diversity—in all its forms—in the classroom.

Recognizing the unique position enabling independent school teachers to push the boundaries of teaching religion/teaching about religion, Brian T. Blackmore offers an experimental pedagogical innovation that provocatively explores how pedagogies of experiential learning intersect with literacy-building about religious and spiritual practices. Could and should students learn about daily Muslim prayer practices by setting five daily alarms on their smart phones? Could students design a sacred, "seder-like" meal focused on social justice and learn something about Judaism? Are such classroom exercises forms of cultural and religious appropriation? What would such Esperanto-like "religious rituals" actually teach students? Who is the teacher in these classroom scenarios? Is the teacher a kind of "preacher" of a neutered/universally accessible religion? Blackmore's essay invites such challenging questions, and affirms the importance of having independent school educators, who occupy a liminal position in the American educational landscape, participate in these conversations.

Similarly, Renee L. Bowling, writing on the project of developing a post-colonial approach religious education in an American Christian missionary school in Asia, is working in a context where the religious positionality of the teacher and the students is being actively explored as the school reevaluates the aims of religious education.

While deeply influenced by American Christianity, the diversity of religious identities of teachers and students alike is being taken into account, resulting in a de-centering (but not abandonment) of missionary Christianity. The binary limits of *Abington* & *Hosana-Tabor* (teacher is/is not a preacher) do not apply to Christian American missionary schools abroad. Hence, in the schema I am proposing here, Bowling's reflections on this dynamic educational context are more akin to American independent schools.

When religion is the classroom subject, what role should the teacher play? As my schema suggests, this question has more than one answer. America is a land of abundance when it comes to approaches to developing religious literacy and interreligious understanding. Christine Gallagher affirms the importance of gathering public school, religious school, and independent school educators together to talk about their different experiences with religious diversity in their classrooms. Institutional and legal expectations with regard to "teaching religion" differ from those regarding "teaching about religion." In her work at an educational nonprofit in Baltimore—the Institute for Islamic, Christian, and Jewish Studies (ICJS), where I serve as Executive Director—Gallagher creates space for teachers to reflect on their own positionality on religion in the classroom in an intensive, ten-month fellowship. The fellowship is designed to help teachers identify and claim their approach to religion and religious diversity in the classroom that is appropriate for their context. Importantly, Gallagher argues that their professional discernment should take account of their own personal relationship to religion, then should explore how that impacts their teaching.

## ON THE EDGES:
## THE IMPORTANCE OF NONPROFIT AND SCHOOL-ADJACENT ORGANIZATIONS

In the development of different approaches to education around religion and religious difference, there is indeed an important role for nonprofit and school-adjacent organizations. Several of the essays in this volume have offered detailed descriptions of diverse initiatives that demonstrate the variety of ways this work can be done, outside of the classroom with students who opt-in to such initiatives. What I found interesting was the range of their hoped-for outcomes for these programs.

Two chapters described interreligious initiatives that were designed to improve school culture and campus climate: Taha Vahanvaty explained the development of a student-led youth acceptance programing at Pennsylvania high schools; Gregory McGonigle detailed chaplaincy-led college transition programs at Tufts University and Emory University. Another three chapters focused on programs that seek to bring religious perspectives to civic issues and social justice work: Lindsay Bressman wrote about Civic Spirit; Megan Hopkins of Mosaic Interfaith Youth Action talked about several justice-oriented experiential interreligious learning programs; Kathleen St. Villier Hill introduced an innovative high school program created by a U.S. congressman to advance Black-Jewish relations in the greater Baltimore region and to provide leadership training and mentorship for students in his district. Considerable creativity and care went into the design of each of these "opt-in" interreligious education initiatives. Their success indicates that students are willing to invest free time in interreligious opportunities.

## NEXT STEPS

Do we have the political will to engage in religious literacy education needed for a religiously diverse democracy? How do we equip citizens and neighbors to better engage their deepest disagreements—particularly when differences are profound and difficult to reconcile? Religious differences cannot be ignored in this vital civic work. Secondary school teachers have an important role to play in it. In short, we need more religion-talk in America's classrooms—and teachers, students, and parents alike need help in making that possible.

In the United States, both education and religion are decentralized. Recognizing that there is not a one-size-fits-most approach is key to envisioning a different future. As the essays gathered in *Interreligious Studies and Secondary Education: Pedagogies and Practices for Living and Learning in a Religiously Plural World* have shown us, creating diverse opportunities for teachers to explore these issues is necessary and important work. Nearly a century after *Scopes*, external pressures, public scrutiny, and institutional demands on teachers continue. But as this volume shows, teachers are creatively reimagining the role of religion in the classroom that takes account of religious and moral diversity. We need to ask more teachers the question: "What is your relationship to religion, and how does it impact your teaching?" And then we need to listen carefully to their answers. I hope the analytical framework offered here can help us appreciate and understand the myriad ways that American teachers engage religion today.

# NOTES

1. State of Tennessee v. John Thomas Scopes (1925).

2. Butler Act (Section 49–1922 of the Tennessee Code Annotated). Tennessee teachers were not allowed to teach evolution in schools until this act was repealed in 1967. You can see the official repeal of the Butler Act at the Tennessee Virtual Archive: https://teva.contentdm.oclc.org/digital/collection/scopes/id/175/.

3. The ACLU had placed advertisements in Tennessee newspapers seeking teachers willing to test the Butler Act in court. John Scopes was a substitute teacher in Dayton, Tennessee and town leaders thought that a sensational trial would put the town on the map. They approached Scopes to see if he would be willing to be indicted for teaching evolution. He agreed.

4. School District of Abington Township, Pennsylvania v. Schempp, 374 US 203 (1963).

5. Sarah Imhoff. "The Creation Story, or How We Learned to Stop Worrying and Love Schempp." *Journal of the American Academy of Religion* 84, no. 2 (June 2016): 466–97.

6. Hosanna-Tabor Evangelical Lutheran Church and School v. EEOC, 565 US 171 (2012).

7. In the United States, Protestant Christianity has been a dominant force in shaping American society as well as informing the conceptual framework for "legal religion." I am using the phrase "teacher as preacher" to reflect that history. See the various publications by Winnifred Fallers Sullivan on the politics of religious freedom.

8. In Roman Catholic tradition, a catechism is both a teaching tool and a resource or reference about Christian truths. It is designed to facilitate education and understanding to faithful Catholics. The most recent version approved by the Vatican was published in 1992. In the United States, the most well-known version is the Baltimore Catechism, which dates from 1885, thus does not reflect teaching from the Second Vatican Council (1962–1965). The United States Conference of Catholic Bishops provides a helpful FAQ about catechism, available online.

9. Rule #1— "...if we begin a sentence with 'this religion believes,' we should assume that the end of that sentence is 'except for all the practitioners who don't.'" Rule #2— "...no one is ever wrong about their religion and their faith."

10. Kennedy v. Bremerton School District, 597 US (2022).

# ABOUT THE EDITORS

*Lucinda Mosher* is Professor of Interreligious Studies at Hartford International University for Religion and Peace, the senior editor of the *Journal of Interreligious Studies*, and the rapporteur of Building Bridges Seminar (an international dialogue of Christian and Muslim scholars). An award-winning editor, her teaching, research, and numerous publications address multireligious concerns in conversation with theology, ethics, and the arts.

*Axel Takács* is an Assistant Professor of Comparative Theology and Interreligious Studies at Seton Hall University and the Editor-in-Chief of the *Journal of Interreligious Studies*. He focuses on Arabic and Persian post-classical Islamic intellectual and poetic traditions as well as comparative theological aesthetics, theopoetics, and theologies of the imagination.

*Christine Gallagher* is head of programs and program director for teachers and schools at the Institute for Islamic, Christian, and Jewish Studies (ICJS) in Baltimore, Maryland. She works with educators, schools, and district offices to think about how religion is present in curriculum and student interactions, with the goal of supporting school communities as they work to dismantle religious bias and bigotry. Before coming to ICJS, she was a classroom teacher in Baltimore.

# ABOUT THE CONTRIBUTORS

**Brian T. Blackmore** is the Director of Quaker Engagement at the American Friends Service Committee and formerly the Religion Department Chair at Westtown School. He holds a Ph.D. in Religious Studies from Temple University and he facilitates workshops about best practices for teaching about religion(s) in independent schools with the Center for Spiritual and Ethical Education.

**Renee L. Bowling** is an international education administrator and a researcher affiliated with The Ohio State University's College Impact Lab. She holds a Ph.D. in Educational Studies, a post-graduate certificate in Religion and Education, and a Master of Arts degree in Counseling and Human Development.

**Lindsay Bressman** holds master's degrees in Social Work and Public Health. She is a community chaplain for all religions, beliefs, and spiritual backgrounds. She participates in the "We Are All Brooklyn Fellowship Against Hate" with the Jewish Community Relations Council and Office for the Prevention of Hate Crimes. Lindsay built Civic Spirit which Facilitates relationships across diverse faith communities through the power of civics education. Lindsay is the Board Chair for Shomer Collective and serves the 67th Precinct Clergy Council for Gun Violence Prevention.

**John Camardella** is a teacher at Prospect High School outside of Chicago, where he created the first dual-credit religious studies course in the United States. He also serves as an RPL Education Fellow at Harvard Divinity School and as a Curriculum Developer for the International Baccalaureate Diploma Programme.

**Chase de Saint-Félix** holds a Master of Arts degree in Philosophy and Social Policy. He is an adjunct instructor in the Department of Philosophy and Religion at American University. He has taught high school history, religion, and ethics in the Baltimore area. His professional writing focuses on teaching religion in secondary educational environments.

**David Michael Avram Gregory** is the owner-operator of Ora et Labora Wine Shop in Portland, Oregon. Prior to this entrepreneurial stint, he taught theology in Catholic high schools. He holds a B.A. from Georgetown University, an M.A. from the Claremont School of Theology, and an Ed.D. from Portland State University.

*Travis Henschen* is an Assistant Principal in the Upper School at the Friends School of Baltimore, where he also teaches history. He holds degrees in School Leadership and in International Studies with a focus on the Middle East.

*Kathleen St. Viller Hill* is the Executive Director of the Elijah Cummings Youth Program in Israel (ECYP) where she ovesees a two-year fellowship program for teens started by the late Congressman Elijah Cummings. Teens in ECYP develop skills that help them become leaders who promote inter-ethnic, racial, and religious understanding, Kathleen holds a Master of Arts degree in Community Education and Leadership.

*Megan Hopkins* is the former Director of Education and Outreach at Mosaic: Interfaith Youth Action. She is currently a Ph.D. Candidate in Comparative Theology at Boston College, where her work focuses on ritual practices in Islam and Christianity, contemplative theologies, and disability theology.

*Eleni Lampadarios* is a teacher at Friends School of Baltimore where she teaches courses covering the history of the modern world and the U.S. She holds a master's degree in Regional Studies—Russia, Eastern Europe, and Central Asia.

*Gregory W. McGonigle* is the University Chaplain and Dean of Religious Life at Emory University in Atlanta, where he has built a multifaith chaplain team and an Interfaith Center. He served in similar roles at UC Davis, Oberlin, and Tufts. He is a Unitarian-Universalist minister and holds degrees in religious studies and divinity from Brown, Harvard, and Boston University.

*Christopher Murray* is a National Board Certified teacher in Montgomery County Maryland where he taught world religions and Religious Literacy for Educators. He holds a B.A. in History from Randolph-Macon College. He lives in Rockville, MD with his wife and two sons.

*Brendan O'Kane* currently serves as President at Mount de Sales Academy in Macon, GA. Previously, he was the Director of Ignatian Mission and Identity at Loyola Blakefield in Towson, MD. He holds master's degrees in Educational Leadership and Theological Studies from Loyola University Maryland.

*Heather Miller Rubens* is the Executive Director and Roman Catholic Scholar at the Institute for Islamic, Christian, and Jewish Studies (ICJS). In her research and writing, Dr. Rubens creatively focuses on the theoretical, theological, ethical, and political implications of affirming religious diversity and building a multireligious democracy. She is currently working on a book entitled *In Good Faith: An Argument for the Interreligious Society.*

*Vicki A. Scullion* holds a doctorate in Teacher Education from the University of Georgia. She is currently studying how religious discrimination is experienced by non-Christian teachers in American public schools.

*John Shekitka* is an Assistant Professor of Secondary Education in the School of Education at Manhattanville University where he has taught since 2018. He is also a part-time visiting professor with the Institute of Education at the American University of Central Asia in Bishkek, Kyrgyzstan. John earned his Ph.D. in the teaching of social studies from Teachers College, Columbia University.

*Taha Vahanvaty* is a student at American University in Washington, DC. He studies law and religion with a focus on intrafaith Islamic dialogue and bridge building within the global Muslim community.

www.ingramcontent.com/pod-product-compliance
Lightning Source LLC
Chambersburg PA
CBHW071737120626
46550CB00002B/551